Mike Meyer

WORK and WIN
with an EXECUTIVE COACH

Maximize Your Opportunity for Exponential Growth

WORK AND WIN WITH AN EXECUTIVE COACH

Copyright © 2019 by Mike Meyer

All rights reserved. No part of this book may be reproduced in any form whatsoever, by photography or xerography or by any other means, by broadcast or transmission, by translation into any kind of language, by recording electronically or otherwise, without permission in writing from the author, except by a reviewer, who may quote brief passages in critical articles or reviews.

ISBN: 978-0-9981779-3-9

Printed in the United States of America

Designed by Ivan Stojic

First Printing: 2019

This is a work of non-fiction. However, I have changed the names and identifying characteristics of many of the individuals in this book to disguise their identities.

www.ArtisanDigital.org
(651) 600-0178

Table of Contents

Praise for *Work and Win with an Executive Coach* 5

PART ONE 9

CHAPTER 1
Why This Book? 11

CHAPTER 2
What Is Executive Coaching? 23

CHAPTER 3
What Will I Get Out of Coaching? 35

CHAPTER 4
What Is the ROI of Coaching? 49

CHAPTER 5
Are You Ready for Coaching? 61

PART TWO 73

CHAPTER 6
Master the Coaching Process 75

CHAPTER 7
Select the Right Coach 91

CHAPTER 8
Nail the Details 107

CHAPTER 9
Get Feedback 121

CHAPTER 10
Create Your Development Plan 135

CHAPTER 11
Make Change Stick 149

CHAPTER 12
Stay on Track 165

Appendix 179

Acknowledgements 201

Praise for *Work and Win with an Executive Coach*

I have seen the impact the right coach can have on a willing business leader. It takes the right attitude and the right coach. Mike knows this firsthand as a former global HR leader and now as a coach himself. His book destigmatizes coaching and is perfect for any executive offered a coaching experience.

Doug Baker
Chairman and CEO, Ecolab

I love this book! It's a pragmatic guide to executive coaching; you'll get the straight story on when a coach can benefit you and how to get the most out of coaching.

Laura Gillund
Chief Talent Officer, Cardiovascular Solutions, Inc.

Not only does **Work and Win** offer practical advice for motivated leaders, but it also provides great guidance for executive coaches who want to learn the "gold standard."

Scott Peterson
EVP and Chief Human Resources Officer, The Schwan Food Company

Full of great insights and helpful tips. This book is incredibly valuable for leaders who are looking to grow professionally.

Bruce Besanko
CFO, Kohl's

This insightful guide brings clarity to all aspects of executive coaching and will ensure you maximize your benefits from coaching. It's a great read for board members, C-Suite executives, HR, and talent development leaders.

Walt Chesley
Chief Human Resources Officer, Hennepin Health

Mike offers an artful and accessible outline of the whens, hows, and whys of executive coaching. **Work and Win** provides a comprehensive road map from selecting the right coach to making new behaviors stick. It is a must-read for executives considering a coach AND for those wanting to get the most out of an existing coaching relationship. For CHROs looking to maximize the return on a coaching investment, **Work and Win** should be required reading!

Christine Webster Moore
Chief Human Resources Officer, Allina Health

Ambitious leaders looking to maximize their impact, performance, and contributions will benefit from having an experienced, independent, and constructive partner along on their journey to success. This engaging book, full of useful examples, will help you capitalize on your relationship with a coach. Mike dispels the myths, stigma, and erroneous assumptions associated with executive coaching.

John Vegas
EVP and Chief Human Resources Officer, Unifi;
Former CHRO, G&K Services

As an executive and a coach, Mike finds a way to get the best out of people. He certainly helped me become a better leader. His pragmatic approach outlined in this book breaks through the noise with no-nonsense counsel. Even if you're not working with a coach, this book will help you be a better leader.

Ryan Festerling
President, QPS Employment;
Former EVP and Chief Human Resource Officer, Kohl's

PART ONE

CHAPTER ONE

Why This Book?

> *I've got to admit it's getting better,*
> *a little better all the time.*
> – Lennon and McCartney

I wasn't the only person in our company battered by the storm stirred up by a senior executive. This guy managed by rage. He lied. He let his people twist in the wind. Our firm's CEO and COO had intentionally positioned me as a direct report to this tornadic leader. My role was to act as buffer, interpreter, and diplomat between him and the rest of the organization.

This executive was acutely focused on consolidating power, and my following within the organization made me a threat. At the time, my skillset didn't include going toe-to-toe with an Alpha Bully Control Freak—the ABC of bad management. Me? I was a master of bringing people together and finding middle ground. I believed that dialog could usually lead everyone to the right answer. In this situation, my strength became weakness, and our ongoing squalls fueled a larger storm.

I needed help.

I ruled out appealing to the CEO, who had chosen my boss rather than me for the role, or to the COO, who would listen sympathetically and then say it was up to me to resolve it. I didn't want to aggravate the situation by venting unproductively to others.

Seeing no room to navigate, I felt stuck. I didn't want to leave the company I loved, and a large financial incentive awaited if I could endure a couple more years.

I muddled through, staying out of Mr. Malignant's line of sight whenever possible. I did my best to protect a far-flung team and to guard myself and family from calamity. Eventually, when another opportunity within the company came along, I escaped.

Looking back, I could have used assistance

— *seeing how my own beliefs and actions contributed to the problem*
— *sorting through my values and priorities*
— *creating a range of options, and*
— *rehearsing the difficult, necessary conversations I avoided*

When I most needed help, I didn't find it.

I survived. Barely. The hard way.

There could have been a better way.

I really needed a coach.

I'm not out to rail against bad managers. I've had a couple dozen bosses, all but one good, several outstanding. Working for or with or over difficult people is just one area where a coach can be helpful. Of course, if you're a boss with issues, a coach can address that too.

My goal in the chapters ahead is to explain when and how a coach can be beneficial and let you in on the secrets of working and winning with a coach. Rather than leave you twisting in workplace winds, I want to help you thrive.

What About You?

What are your pain points at work?

Where are your edges too sharp—or not sharp enough?

How frequently do you get real, honest, constructive feedback on elements where you can improve?

Who holds you accountable for progress?

Who can expertly guide you in your professional development, steadfastly stand on your side, and purposefully partner with you?

Maybe you're wondering if a board member or boss could fill that role. Or someone on your team. A peer or mentor. Your spouse. Maybe your dog. While each of those choices have potential, all likely lack one or more key attributes essential to guiding you, whether you need objectivity, experience, knowledge, or wisdom. A good executive coach has all the attributes you need in a development ally: perspective, proficiency, expertise, and sound judgment.

With an executive coach, you can accomplish more than you can on your own to grow and develop, become a better leader, and dodge pitfalls along the way.

That is why executive coaching is becoming prevalent in organizations of all kinds, including businesses, non-profits, government, and educational institutions. People come to executive coaching in different ways and for different reasons. Some receive coaching as part of a training program or in conjunction with assimilation to a new organization. Others are told they need fine-tuning and pull in a coach to speed their progress. A few get an ultimatum about their performance, and they're sent to a coach to help them climb out of a hole.

Some real-life examples, with details altered to protect identity:

- Robert fell back into his office, reeling from his boss's words. Stephanie claimed everything was going fine yet wanted him to partner with a coach on his "executive presence." Robert, a seasoned VP of Strategy in a large industrial corporation, wasn't certain what an executive coach did, but he was sure this wasn't good. Weren't coaches a last-ditch attempt to fix people? And nobody had ever told Robert he lacked executive presence, whatever that was. HR was expecting Robert's call and would help him identify a coach.

- Amy, an IT SVP at a global bank, was invited to join a prestigious internal leadership development program. The plan consisted of three weeks of classroom training, team building, group projects, self-assessment, and coaching. Amy was honored to participate, though she felt unsure about the coaching component. She had never worked with a coach and didn't like the thought of being analyzed. Given the company's atmosphere of backchannel communications, she was concerned about confidentiality.

- Anthony anticipated a tough annual performance appraisal. He had been promoted to General Manager for Mining a year prior, and during that time, the industry had been rocked by unprecedented oversupply. Prices had careened downward. Customers were declaring bankruptcy and negotiating extended terms. The COO sharply criticized his GM's lack of aggressive action and implied that without significant improvement, Anthony would be out of a job before long. The COO had engaged a coach to move Anthony forward.

- Andrea had just joined a large insurance outfit as new head of group plans. Her move from another industry and relocation from the East to the Midwest made for a big decision that took almost six months to close. She had already found her new company far more culturally conservative than her previous employer. In addition, assuming responsibility for a full P&L brought more pressure than her prior accountability for sales. Finally, the move itself multiplied challenges. As part of the final deal, she requested a coach to help her assimilate into the new company and role.

- Jerome learned in his performance review that he was in the succession pool for general management roles in his current company. This had been one of Jerome's career objectives for years, and he was excited to get confirmation of his potential. However, his boss also mentioned he needed to develop to reach this level, including work on thinking more strategically and leading more powerfully and authentically. Coaching was available if he was interested, and HR could provide details.

Maybe you see yourself in these situations. Or coaching might be on your radar for completely different reasons.

I'm counting on one thing. If you've picked up this book, you're likely hungry to learn, grow, and make a difference. You want to keep moving. And you know you need to move faster than the world around you. Whatever the reason, working with a coach can be an opportunity to be a better leader, intentionally and exponentially.

Success Ahead

I've spent my career observing what makes leaders successful.

I led the HR function for a $14 billion Fortune 250 company with 45,000 employees in 70 countries.

I've been a global leader on multiple continents, including running HR in Asia and a cardiac device business in Latin America.

I've seen coaches propel executives to greater success.

As a senior HR executive, I vetted and hired coaches for other senior executives. I've been coached myself. For the last several years, I've coached senior executives at large- and mid-sized companies from Singapore to the United States to Switzerland.

Over my varied career, I've observed executives who were fantastic and others who flamed out. I've seen what it takes for leaders to

—— *get people to follow them*
—— *get results*
—— *get promoted*
—— *get to a place where they thrive*

Success comes from cultivating positive attributes, which have been copiously catalogued by my HR colleagues and me in competency models encompassing experience, knowledge, and behavior. Success also comes from mitigating negative tendencies. A multitude of psychological assessments can reveal leadership derailers that can cause a leader to skip the tracks—traits like abrasiveness, poor listening, indecisiveness, micromanagement, and emotional outbursts.

What drives everything forward, however, is a singular personal success factor, the secret sauce that turns the competency stew into bouillabaisse. It's so simple it's easy to overlook. Because you've picked up this book, I'm confident you already possess it to some degree:

Success results from openness—a willingness, perhaps an eagerness—to change.

Change isn't easy. You might be the exception, but most people find it difficult to make—and sustain—substantive changes in attitudes and behaviors. Later in this book, I'll explain why. But I fully believe it's possible for anyone with an openness to change to develop and grow. It takes the right combination of

—— **challenging work**, supplemented by
—— **specific learning**, along with
—— **select people** as catalysts

Ideally, all three—challenge, learning, and people—are integrated to spur you forward. And at key points in your career, a person—boss, mentor, or coach—can be the catalyst bringing the other ingredients together into a cohesive whole.

I became an executive coach years ago because I observed again and again that good coaches have the chops to partner with an amazing diversity of talented, interesting people. They step into situations and advance development in profound ways. I'm convinced that a competent coach can help you harness your work challenges and incorporate new learning to produce lasting improvement in your effectiveness. You can count on a good coach as a trusted member of your team, your personal board of advisers.

Why This Book?

Organizations spend $2 billion each year to provide professional coaching to over 500,000 executives, according to a 2016 study for the International Coach Federation conducted by the leading consulting firm PWC. Those numbers are projected to grow up to 10% annually. Executive coaching costs $15,000 to $30,000 or more for each executive, who must also commit to up to a year of regular meetings, homework, and feedback. Even though the process is confidential, it's likely visible throughout an organization. People know if you're working with a coach.

Clients put money, time, and their own reputations on the line.

What's surprising is how this sizable investment is often made blindly. Imagine buying a new car without research or a test drive. Until now, coaching has been concealed in a black box with little light shining in on what really happens and what creates results. This lack of information hinders executives from taking ownership of what might be the single largest developmental investment of their working years.

Like any area where you draw on another's expertise—an attorney, physician, personal trainer, or financial adviser—it pays to understand the formula for success. Your goal is to pick the right partner—one you can trust with something as critical as your career—and make sure you get the results you want.

Regardless of the context that has brought YOU to coaching, you likely have questions and concerns about working with an executive coach:

- What is executive coaching?
- When should I engage a coach?
- How do I select a coach?
- What does the process of coaching look like?
- What happens in a coaching session?
- How does confidentiality work, and what information gets reported back to my employer?
- How long does this process last, and how do I sustain my results once I've finished the formal coaching?
- What can I realistically expect to gain from coaching?
- How can I make sure I maximize the opportunity?

Many people start out skeptical of coaching, and with good reason. Anyone can build a website, print business cards, and call themselves a coach. No certification required. Zero barriers to entry.

As a result, coaches vary wildly in training, experience, and quality. It's therefore perhaps even more important to be as thoughtful and deliberate in selecting your professional development partner as in choosing a doctor, or lawyer, or financial adviser—professionals trained in standardized curricula, credentialed by recognized authorities, and governed by strict legalities.

Helping you choose the right coach is one of goals of this book, so you aren't left wondering, "Who is *that person* to advise me or claim to understand how to advance my career?"

I wouldn't blame you for having other reservations. I'll even suggest some. We might as well get them out in the open right now:

- I don't need therapy.

- I don't have time.

- I've been successful doing what I do. Why change?

- I don't want to get into touchy-feely stuff.

- I really don't like talking about myself.

And many leaders have this underlying anxiety:

- I fear what coaching says about my effectiveness as an executive.

Dispelling these myths is another aim of this book.

What Next?

I want you to get as much out of coaching as you can.

Understanding the potential benefits of working with a coach will help you do just that. Coaching is a powerful solution to many challenges leaders face. But it isn't for everyone. And it isn't for every situation. We will explore where coaching is most effective, and where you might consider other development approaches instead of, or in addition to, coaching.

There are hundreds of books written about coaching. What makes this one different is that **it's written for you, the client**—the person being coached, or considering it. I'll cut through the hype and jargon so you clearly understand what lies ahead. I don't want to turn you into a coach, just an educated client.

You'll learn the truth about executive coaching, just as you'll learn many truths about yourself in the coaching process. Bottom line? I'll give you the tools and information you need to take control of your coaching program and get the highest possible return on this pivotal experience.

CHAPTER ONE—KEY QUESTIONS

Before you turn to the next chapter, I want to pitch you a few key questions, a pattern I'll follow throughout this book's first section.

Think through each of the queries below. Jot a few words here or grab your favorite device or diary and answer at length. Either way, you'll get introduced to an experience of executive coaching that will get you ready for your one-on-one engagement.

- At what points in your career could you have profited from an outside expert's objectivity, knowledge, experience, perspective, and wisdom?

- Why are you considering working with a coach?

- What do you hope a coach can do for you that you can't do for yourself?

- What concerns do you have about working with a coach?

- What questions do you need answered before you move ahead?

- If you were to engage with a coach, what best possible outcomes would you like to achieve?

CHAPTER TWO

What Is Executive Coaching?

> *Coaches live in the air...live in the ear...*
> *they want you better than you are...*
>
> – James Dickey, "The Bee,"
> a poem about his Clemson football coach

I was at the gym cooling down post-workout when a young man, he of impossibly big biceps, approached me to say he had overheard me mention I was a coach.

He was looking for coaching!

When I explained that I wasn't an athletic but rather an executive coach and explained what that meant, he seemed confused and then disappointed.

When executives think of coaches, they usually picture sports coaches—tightly-wound, regimented men and women roving the sidelines and yelling with exasperation at their athletes. In our everyday imaginations, real coaches tell people what to do. They scribble plays. They take charge of outwitting and outgunning the competition. They rule their domain.

I like athletic coaches. They've personally taught me more than a trick or two I use every day of my life. These experts know their game and the buttons to push to motivate others. Moreover, most athletic coaches are courageously visible, with their successes and failures easily measured by the scoreboard, flashing numbers hyper-analyzed by fans and armchair commentators.

This isn't how executive coaches roll.

Of course, there are basic similarities. Between "games," the athletic coach and the executive coach analyze their coachees and devise plans to enhance skills, sharpen thinking, and increase the probability of winning.

From there, significant differences emerge.

Almost all athletic coaching is hierarchical, while the executive coaching relationship is a powerful partnership of equals.

An athletic coach is often forcefully directive. The executive coach is a trained, experienced professional with the requisite expertise to come alongside the client on a journey with development as its destination.

You can expect an executive coach to

- Listen intently

- Serve up far more questions than answers

- Execute a game plan intentionally designed to flex and adapt

- Appear on the field rarely if ever, except perhaps to shadow a client at meetings or presentations—and even then, to observe silently and provide perspective later in private. And no yelling or screaming with looks of anger or disgust!

Coaches are thought partners who help clients generate options and ideas to address challenges. They're keen observers who get clients to see what they might otherwise miss. They're guides to the process of professional growth. They understand business and organizational dynamics. They're savvy adult development experts with the moxie to elicit change. To many clients, they're accountability partners.

In an executive coaching session, the coach gets at the heart of the challenge the client is facing. Yet for the most part, it's the client who identifies needs and potential actions, not the coach.

As I work with my clients, I'm listening more than talking. I'm curious. I want to understand how the client views the world and gauges his or her effectiveness in it. I ask a lot of questions, mostly for the client, to uncover a new perspective or approach that might be more effective than the current one. I'm careful not to ask leading questions that prompt a pre-determined response. I'm on the edge of my seat as I watch the client search inside for answers.

Coaching is future-oriented. It focuses on the individual at work. It's largely about behavior, although it often addresses limiting beliefs that keep people from achieving their best.

Although the core of executive coaching happens in a two-person partnership of coach and client, at strategic points the program typically incorporates other key players. Right at the start, we usually bring in the client's manager or other sponsor to help determine coaching outcomes. Early in the process, we often solicit feedback from colleagues. After several months, we check in with the boss to exchange information on client progress. Toward the end of the engagement, we might again check in with others to assess progress.

What Executive Coaching Isn't

As I start with some clients, I see anxiety about being coached in their eyes and the furrows of their brow. I don't delve into bad childhood experiences, like playing ball under a crazy coach. I just address the nervousness that usually stems from inaccurate assumptions or secondhand opinions about coaches and coaching.

So let's clear up some misconceptions. Executive coaching is commonly confused with therapy, with consulting, and with mentoring. Given the overlap between these disciplines, it's easy to see why. As you consider engaging a coach, you should understand what you'll get—or not get—if you sign up for the program. You want to know you're selecting the right professional and process for your situation.

Coaching isn't therapy.

I've had clients refer to me as "my therapist." Believe me, I'm not a therapist and don't practice therapy on my clients. But I get their point. When we close the door and a session begins, they've entered a place where it's safe to talk about anything. We can explore. They can vent (five-minute limit!). All with no judgment on my part. I just stay curious.

Therapy is an experience different in degree and kind. Counselors delve into topics coaches don't touch. You should have no fear that a coach wants to know your deepest feelings on a personal topic or to probe past experiences that haunt you. That can be important stuff—that is, in the right setting with a thoroughly trained mental health provider.

> **Therapists** focus more on the past and try to diagnose and heal dysfunction. Therapy is normally billed to the individual or to insurance, while coaching is normally paid by the organization.

I've had clients who might have benefited from therapy in addition to coaching, or from therapy instead of coaching. Coaches are trained to make referrals to mental health professionals in situations that call for it. Once when a client shared he had recently lost a sister to cancer and also faced two challenging teens at home, I wondered aloud if he had considered counseling. "Don't worry," he said. "I already have a therapist!" In another situation, I realized my client was struggling with substance abuse, and I offered to refer her to a trusted therapist or program. Other coaches I know have addressed even more serious situations. They referred the client to get appropriate help.

Coaching isn't consulting.

Sometimes a coaching client asks for my views, judgment, or opinion on a business issue. Coaches are trained NOT to go down that path. They instead employ powerful questions to prompt the client to answer these questions for himself or herself. The assumption is that the client knows far more about the situation than a coach ever can. We're here to bring out solutions that already reside somewhere within.

Now, I do have extensive experience as a business executive. Occasionally, after exhausting a client's range of ideas, options, and perspectives, I offer my own. Sometimes the client asks for it, sometimes they don't. I go so far as to ask for permission even when the client has specifically requested my point of view. I then pretend to take off my coaching hat and put on my consulting hat, miming the actions and telling the client what I'm doing. Only then do I briefly speak as a consultant. And then I put my coaching hat back on.

> **Consultants** analyze and recommend solutions to specific enterprise challenges or opportunities. They rarely advise executives on behavioral issues like leadership style or potential derailers.

Coaching isn't mentoring.

In my past life as an HR executive, I served as a formal and informal mentor to many more junior people. I also established mentoring programs to match mentors with protégés and give structure to mentoring relationships. Mentors were selected for their expertise in a technical arena, in leadership, or in navigating the company. They gave advice to their charges in these areas yet weren't expected to provide executive development expertise. The relationships and meetings were less formal and frequent than typical coaching engagements.

> **Mentors** provide advice, guidance, or training for more junior people in an organization.

Unlike mentors, executive coaches generally don't provide advice or training in an area even in which they are subject matter experts. Coaches instead provide *guidance on the process and a plan for professional development.* Part of that roadmap may include identifying a mentor for help in specific areas.

I draw these distinctions because it's important to understand what coaching is and isn't. It helps to understand what to expect from these relationships.

What Executive Coaching Is

Yesterday I had a chemistry conversation with a prospective coaching client at a large national insurance company. Like most of my clients, he had never worked with a coach and didn't really understand executive coaching. Here, in a nutshell, is what I told him.

Executive Coaching is:

- **A structured, well-defined process.** Coaching assesses leadership effectiveness and develops an action plan to improve. While the process is flexible and tailored to the situation, there is structure. Specific components and steps can be mixed and matched to suit the circumstances.

- **An intensive, focused effort with a definite beginning and end.** The coaching process has pace and momentum. It has defined outcomes and a timeline for key milestones.

- **A development process with a proven business benefit and measurable outcomes.** As Stephen Covey said, "Begin with the end in mind." The coaching process starts by defining outcomes and builds in checks along the way to ensure client and coach stay on track.

- **A partnership owned by the client.** Later I'll say more about what makes a coaching engagement successful. Underlying everything is client ownership. The client takes accountability for results. The coach empowers the client, avoiding dependency that causes the relationship to persist beyond the point of diminishing returns.

- **An opportunity for exceptional professional growth.** How many times in your career will a company make a significant investment in your development? Probably only once. This is a time for you to focus on you, which at first makes many executives uncomfortable. But the chance for exponential growth doesn't come around often, so why not go for it?

Moving Forward

By describing these similarities and differences you probably know immediately where to turn for help with your specific needs. Most of the time, it's clear as a bluebird day in the Rockies. Table 1 summarizes the differences between coaching, mentoring, therapy, and consulting.

TABLE 1: COACHING, MENTORING, THERAPY, CONSULTING

	Coaching	Mentoring	Therapy	Consulting
Purpose	Improve effectiveness at work	Navigate organization; learn from someone who's "been there"	Diagnose and treat psychological dysfunction	Enhance organization performance or address a business challenge
Process/ Approach	Planned, tailored process with flexibility	Can be structured or more informal	Variety of approaches, depending on provider training and individual needs	Typically use a highly structured approach to analyze and make recommendations

	Coaching	Mentoring	Therapy	Consulting
Person	**Executive coach**—partners in strengthening leadership effectiveness	**More senior executive**—provides advice on how to handle situations	**Psychologist**—asks probing questions to understand past	**Business consultant**—analyzes situation and develops recommendations
Duration	Typically 6-12 months	Varies; typically a year	Open-ended	Project dependent
Outcome	Enhanced leadership effectiveness	Advice on how to handle situations and meet career goals	Internal congruence and personal well-being	Executable plan for addressing a business issue
Focus	Future behavior change	Organizational savvy	Past psychological challenges and impact on present	Business situation
Fee/Payment	Paid by organization	Paid by organization; usually no or low fee	Paid by individual or insurance	Paid by organization

At times, however, the fog rolls in. Your needs, for example, could be addressed by more than one category of professionals:

- A leader who wants help managing stress might seek help from a therapist or a coach.

- An executive wanting to lead an organization through change or a shift in strategy could choose a consultant or a coach.

- Someone looking to develop specific skills or needing help navigating an organization might look to a mentor or a coach.

Other situations could create a mix between your most pressing needs and interests, and some executives find it appropriate to work in tandem with more than one professional. I've had coaching engagements where the client was also seeing a therapist, a few where consultants were also engaged, and many others where clients also had mentors.

If you're debating which way to turn, go back to the purpose of each as outlined above. Talk to a few people in these professions or to others who have dealt with needs similar to yours.

- If you need analysis, recommendations, and advice on a business opportunity or challenge—get a consultant.

- If you need help coping with non-work relationships or with emotional or psychological concerns—get a therapist.

- If you need advice from a senior leader—get a mentor.

- If you need a partner on professional development—get a coach.

The Promise

The demands of being an executive are never-ending, the pressure intense, the schedule 24/7. Your not-so-smart phone pings all night with emails and texts from the far side of the globe. When you finally catch a break for a quick one-night getaway, that solitary weekend with no soccer games, the boss calls on Sunday and wants something from you first thing Monday.

I've sat in that sometimes very uncomfortable Herman Miller chair. But what if you could find real, relevant help?

What if you had someone—always, tenaciously—

—— *on your team?*
—— *working on your behalf?*
—— *focused solely on you?*
—— *helping you accomplish your objectives?*
—— *facilitating your development?*

- supporting you in reaching your career aspirations?
- meeting your most stubborn stare?
- speaking up when you're wrong?
- asking provocative questions?
- forcing you to think deeply and differently?
- serving up concrete suggestions for changes in behavior?
- partnering with you with no personal skin in the game, no axe to grind, beyond wanting you to be even more effective and successful?

The next two chapters will help deepen your understanding of the benefits of executive coaching, the typical areas where coaches step in and help, and the actual business ROI. That additional exploration will help you decide whether to engage a coach—and if you do, encourage you to go all-in and make the most of the experience.

CHAPTER TWO—KEY QUESTIONS

- What key concerns of work or life do you wish you could improve or altogether solve?

- What previously "unsolvable" issue would you like to address—if you could find the right help?

- What are your greatest challenges at work?

- What areas of leadership effectiveness do you wish to strengthen?

- Who could you talk to—coaches, mentors, consultants, therapists, or others—to shed more light on these areas? What questions do you most want answered?

- Who among your colleagues, peers, HR, or friends might have relevant experience they could share with you?

CHAPTER THREE

What Will I Get Out of Coaching?

I want the truth.

– Tom Cruise, A Few Good Men

In my first role as an HR manager, I worked for the newly installed president of a two-billion-dollar business. Shortly after moving into his office, he asked me upstairs for an impromptu conversation. As I entered his suite, I was met by layers of wood paneling, ornate chandeliers, intricately carved furniture, and lavish oil paintings in gilded frames. I froze—although, I admit, something about the thick carpet beckoned me to run barefoot.

The president sat behind a desk seemingly hewn from a single colossal piece of oak burnished to a bright mirror sheen. He motioned for me to sit in a posh red velvet chair with engraved wooden arms.

While the boss was personable, he was soft spoken—almost aloof.

I tried to get my butterflies to fly in formation.

We talked about miscellanea and then he said, "Mike, I need your help."

"Of course. What can I do?"

"I want you to be my coach."

I was stumped. I resided miles below this leader in the corporate structure, and this was long before coaching was a thing.

"How?"

"Mike, yesterday was the last day I heard truth. From now on, everything I get will be filtered by people who tell me what they think I want to hear. That's why I need your feedback. I want you to collect it from others too. I need to know where I'm making a difference and where I'm failing. I would welcome that."

I did what the new president asked, and over time, I watched him embrace even the harshest messages with humor and grace. He obviously welcomed feedback as a gift, responding with thoughtful, almost artful actions.

Ironically, a few months later, the chandelier over the boss's conference table crashed down as he met with an employee particularly ill-prepared to deal with that degree of shock and awe.

Honestly, the oak-encased office wasn't helping the president do his best, and the shattered chandelier brought that point home. A few months later, our leader moved next door into a more modern, less imposing office.

Ye Shall Know the Truth

The higher you rise in an organization, the less likely you hear what's really going on—realities essential to doing your job, Truth with a capital T. In fact, there's an inverse relationship between the level you've attained and people's willingness to speak frankly in your presence.

I can hardly blame those who don't speak up. Risk takers who tell an executive the truth or confront unproductive behavior sometimes get shot at. Publicly. I've been there. It's not fun.

But think back to your last performance review, or 360, or internal conversation about your future. Did you get all the feedback you wanted and needed? Or did you sense important truths were skirted or left altogether unsaid?

Unfortunately, most organizations don't speak truth to people about their performance and growth trajectory. Do you have potential to move up? What box are you in on the succession grid? How do direct reports, peers, and senior leaders really see you? What do external stakeholders say behind your back? What can you do to progress?

There are reasons organizations hold back. The reasons aren't good. But they're understandable.

One reason is flight. If the organization tells employees they've screwed up, or that they have developmental issues or poor performance overall, or that they've topped out, they might exit. Leaving might or might not be a good thing, but it's often inconvenient to the organization.

Simple aversion to conflict is another key reason organizations hold back. Some leaders hide from confrontation. They hate giving honest feedback. They fear a brush-up even when their message is overwhelmingly positive.

Paradoxically, when an organization finds courage to offer constructive criticism, the recipient often doesn't like it, hear it, or absorb it. Leaders at every level manage to slough off the most hard-baked feedback. They're Teflon. Nothing sticks.

Coaches, however, traffic in truth. It's the coach's job to collect feedback and make sure the client hears it.

Coaching Gift One: Truth

Truth is one of two great gifts a coach gives a client.

Occasionally, truth derives from a coach's direct observation of the executive in a session or shadowing the executive in the course of work. Most often, truth comes from data the coach gathers. Even as the coach conveys that information to the executive in a calm, dispassionate, non-threatening manner, the coach doesn't budge, because standing by the message is one of the most valuable benefits a coach can offer. If a coach can't deliver difficult feedback, coaching's power diminishes. If a coach lets you go on thinking all is well in your world when it's not, the return on your investment of time, money, and reputation can be worthless—or worse, if a lack of insight tanks your career.

Truth comes in two flavors:

- *Internal Self-Awareness*
- *External Self-Awareness*

Internal self-awareness results from understanding the unique mix of characteristics that make you *you*—and, by extension, drive your actions. Assessments and feedback elevate your conscious command of your values, beliefs, motivations, and preferences. With greater internal self-awareness, you can understand which work cultures and situations play to your strengths and which might cause you to struggle.

External self-awareness means you see yourself as others do. A coach might solicit feedback from direct reports, peers, your boss, customers, or others through interviews or an online 360. If you take these responses seriously, the external awareness you gain will tell you which behaviors help you achieve your goals and which get in your way.

The aim of increasing self-awareness is to uncover blind spots, which can be positive (strengths you aren't aware of) or negative (weaknesses you aren't aware of). Or you might see with renewed clarity the impact on others of strengths and weaknesses you already know about.

A Window on Yourself

The Johari window, elucidated and cleverly branded by Joseph Luft and Harrington Ingham in the 1950s, calls out known and unknown areas of self, with pointed implications for our growth.

The four quadrants in the Johari window sort every truth about you—whether a fact is known or unknown, by you and by others. Your best response to the truths in each quadrant differs, and a coach will work with information in each to increase your effectiveness as a leader.

	Known to self	Not known to self
Known to others	Public	Blind Spot
	Active response: Gauge effectiveness	*Active response: Get feedback*
Not known to others	Hidden (or "Façade")	Unknown
	Active response: Selective self-disclosure	*Active response: Self-discovery*

In the **PUBLIC quadrant**, your beliefs and behaviors are known by self and others. Your goal, consequently, is to gauge the effectiveness of those behaviors to determine whether they drive the result you intend. If they do, don't change! However, if your usual patterns aren't working as well as you want, you can alter the behaviors or underlying beliefs (more on that later). A coach will help you assess the effectiveness of your actions, determine what no longer serves you, and partner with you on a plan for change.

In the **BLIND SPOT quadrant**, the coach starts by gathering and presenting information to make you aware of what was previously hidden from you. Blind spots can be underutilized strengths. Others might be unseen impediments. Armed with this information, you can act, again working with a coach to develop your plan.

In the **HIDDEN quadrant** are facts and feelings you don't want others to know, like fears of being inadequate, being an impostor, or being a fraud. Or looking stupid. Or diminished reputation. A coach, through assessments and dialog, helps you uncover and be more comfortable dealing with the gunk in this quadrant, which presents interesting choices. Increasing your awareness can loosen the grip fear might have on you, reducing your anxiety and enhancing your freedom to act. You might also choose to selectively disclose your fears. I'm not talking about oversharing, but rather planned disclosures that make you more human, approachable, and relatable.

In the **UNKNOWN quadrant** is your subconscious, or as Bogart said in the closing line of the film *The Maltese Falcon*, "the stuff that dreams are made of." Your goal here is to discover what's under your hood and move what you learn into one of the other boxes for processing. Coaches don't go here deliberately, but sometimes stuff pops out—in flashes of intuition, self-awareness, and insight. Suddenly you know something about yourself that hadn't occurred to you before. These discoveries often emerge as a byproduct of addressing other quadrants. The lights are suddenly brighter, even without the help of an exploding chandelier!

Armed with insight, you perceive your blind spots. You wrestle with the values and beliefs that drive your behavior. You better understand your impact on others. All of that new self-awareness adds up to opportunities to act.

Coaching Gift Two: Accountability for Action

Martial artist and aspiring executive coach Bruce Lee said, "Knowing is not enough. We must apply. Willing is not enough. We must do."

As a coach, I'm energized by seeing a client's eyes light up when they spot a truth previously unnoticed. And when a client grasps their impact on others, it's like stadium lights flipping on. Even the parking lot gets illuminated.

Self-awareness is terrific. But I've seen coaches and clients stop there. After all, everyone assumes an executive is smart and effective enough to know how to take information and act. Unfortunately, that almost never happens. When it does, it almost never lasts!

Why?

First, it's not always immediately clear what levers will improve leadership effectiveness. It's vital to generate a list of potential actions, narrow it down, and commit to experiments to test what works.

Second, no amount of spelling out next steps guarantees an executive will take the first step or continue in a new direction. Our human struggle to do right is real, and a classic proof comes in the form of resolutions to get fit and lose weight. On January 2, gym parking lots fill and people wait for equipment. By Groundhog Day, lots are empty and equipment waits for people.

The same phenomenon exists with prescription medication compliance. Fewer than half of people on a cholesterol-lowering regimen refill their prescriptions, even though the regimen can have life-saving or life-extending effects. Even when you know what you need to do, taking and sustaining action isn't easy.

The second gift that a coach gives a client is accountability for action.

My clients are all intensely busy with the demands all executives experience. They seldom rest. They never shut down completely. They need to be corporate athletes, performing at their mental and physical peaks at a moment's notice. They also have families, friends, communities, hobbies, interests, religions, causes. There's no end.

In my executive roles, every day felt like a marathon sprint, running from meeting to meeting, out of breath. Food was optional. A bathroom break meant showing up late for the next meeting.

So where can you find time for the added demands of working with a coach? Sessions take time, and so does homework. You're supposed to try new behaviors, reflect on what to do or what you've done, develop a skill, or read relevant material. Even the mental rigor of thinking new thoughts can drain you.

It's not easy. But for the time you're engaged with the coach, follow-through is imperative. Like anything, what you put into the process determines what you get out.

A good coach can help there, building in accountability.

A coach can teach multiple techniques for increasing the likelihood you'll change and sustain your new behaviors. That starts with simply showing up for the coaching session!

Go back to the gym for a minute. If you have an appointment with a personal trainer—a commitment you pay for—the odds of your showing up increases dramatically. Having a gym buddy works almost as well. I know. I started working out 35 years ago and have continued without quitting. But when I began, I had countless reasons my resolve wouldn't last. Fortunately, I had a buddy who kept me making time for running and the gym—the woman who later became my wife. If she was going, count me in. It started a habit and a marriage that has endured.

Many clients tell me they accomplished a task or tried a behavior because they knew I would ask the next time we met. That's accountability.

There are other ways to build accountability, including goal setting, three-way meetings with your boss, and check-ins with stakeholders. More about sustainability in Chapter 11.

Results You Can See

Great, you might be thinking. *I'll know myself better. I'll understand how others see me. And I'll be more willing and able to change. But what real difference does that make?*

My experience, which is backed up by research, shows nearly three dozen benefits you can expect from coaching.

Typical benefits of coaching to individuals

- Enhanced leadership skills, including:
  - Communication
  - Persuasion
  - Change management
  - Setting vision and strategy
  - Prioritization
  - Execution
  - Organization
  - Driving your agenda
  - Interpersonal skills
  - Trust
  - Collaboration
  - Delegation

- Teambuilding
  - Direct-report development
  - Time management
  - Personal productivity
- More thoughtful and decisive decision-making
- Greater influence and ability to advance initiatives
- Increased ability to read others accurately, whether understanding their motivations, preferences, and abilities or providing work and development uniquely suited to them
- Keener sense of how you are perceived
- Competitive advantages rooted in self-awareness that many rivals lack
- Clearer understanding of blind spots and how to improve
- Feedback you aren't likely to hear from others
- A sounding board to test new ideas and approaches
- A safe place to walk through challenges and work through options
- A collaborative partner to challenge your thinking and help you see the mindsets and values that cause you to behave as you do
- An accountability structure for actions and results
- A partner who calls out habits that undermine your effectiveness
- Help navigating new organizations and cultures

- Alignment of roles and goals with your core preferences, motivations, and values

- Power to identify new behaviors and a place to experiment with and practice them, increasing your range and number of behavioral options

- Greater confidence

- Increased know-how to initiate personal change and continually improve

- Increased self-control, poise, and regulation

- Enhanced resilience under stress, pressure, or that feeling your world is out of control

- Advancement (seriously, I have had several clients promoted while being coached, or soon after!)

Typical benefits of coaching to the organization

- Enhanced business results—sales, profitability, margins, costs, efficiency, and more

- Increased employee engagement

- Reduced turnover

- Improved individual performance

- Improved team performance

- Development of high-growth trajectory employees for future succession

- Proof of organizational commitment to development

- Increased opportunities for individuals to take accountability for their development

- Higher EQ within your organization

- Preempting potential problems

- Stronger onboarding and reduced likelihood of early losses

- Better organizational culture

One of my all-time best bosses is now CEO of one of the world's largest pharmaceutical companies. He was a master at simplifying large amounts of complex information, and among his favorite phrases was one he used to introduce his synthesis. He would say something like this: "At the end of the day, what you can expect from coaching is to accelerate your professional growth and become a significantly more effective leader. You will be better at the end of the process." As another famous CEO might say, "I GUARANTEE IT!"

CHAPTER THREE—KEY QUESTIONS

- Who do you rely on to tell you the truth?

- When does their truth-telling fall short of what you need to be your best?

- Who holds you accountable? How? How effectively?

- Finish this statement:
  "Coaching would be worth my time and effort if I..."

- What benefits are you looking for from coaching?

- What benefits would your organization receive?

- What does "better" look like at the end of the process?

CHAPTER FOUR

What Is the ROI of Coaching?

> *The best moments usually occur when a person's body or mind is stretched to its limits in a voluntary effort to accomplish something difficult and worthwhile.*
>
> – Tal Ben Shahar

Back in the day, a colleague of mine made the front cover of *Fortune Magazine* as one of the early executive coaches. In that era, organizations summoned psychologists when talented yet abrasive or abusive executives needed a dose of reality. As that conveyer of truth, Fred Kiel would interview dozens of people around an executive, not only boss, peers, and direct reports but also spouse, children, and neighbors. In a wrenching two-day session, Fred would give the executive the bad news: Here's how you behave, and here's how it impacts those around you.

It was an intervention, really. Nothing was held back. The executive got what might be a last-ditch opportunity to see the destructiveness of their actions and the peril of losing everything they cared about. The goal of truth-telling was to get the executive to recognize significant, dramatic, transformational change as their only option.

Fast forward more than 30 years.

Gone are the days of coach as investigator and interrogator, when having a coach undoubtedly meant you were in trouble.

While coaches still address remedial situations, it's rare. Organizations are less likely to be patient or invest in difficult leaders. Most companies feel better about spending money on people already performing well who, given the right catalyst, will contribute at even higher levels. Fred went on to write a pair of acclaimed books on leadership character, a topic now at the core of his work. And executive coaching has evolved to address a wide variety of needs.

Coaching by the Numbers

Studies by both the *Harvard Business Review* and PriceWaterhouseCoopers (on behalf of the International Coach Federation) show how much coaching has changed:

- No more than 10-15% of coaches report being engaged to address derailing behaviors.

- The majority of coaching engagements aim to develop high potentials for future opportunities or to deepen the pool of successors.

- This dominant category of positive engagements also includes coaching for on-boarding, helping a new leader assimilate into company culture. This is a compelling response to data showing that 40% of executives hired from the outside fail within their first 18 months.

- About a quarter of coaching engagements are designed to provide the executive with a sounding board, most often initiated when the leader needs to guide the organization through dramatic change.

With coaches being called in to address an increasing breadth of situations, the coaching industry is booming, and coaches are ubiquitous in large- and medium-sized organizations. Business coaches now number 20,000 in North America, with another 30,000 spread around the world. Coaches responding to the PWC survey reported an average of 11 active clients, translating to more than a half million coaching engagements. Significantly, coaching is now a $2.4 billion+ industry globally, with about $1 billion spent in North America and a similar amount in Europe. Ten percent annual growth is expected over the next few years, keeping pace with the recent past.

The boom brings challenges. Key among them from a buyer's point of view: The diverse reasons coaches engage with clients make outcomes increasingly difficult to quantify.

I've already mentioned the importance of linking coaching objectives to business value. That might seem obvious, but plenty of coaches neglect to have that all-important discussion at the outset, at least with the client and likely with the client's manager as well. At the beginning of my engagements, I work with client and boss to identify tangible, specific outcomes and discuss the impact these changes will have on the business.

In Table 2, I identify the five most common executive coaching scenarios with their key business value. I'll comment on the ROI math below.

TABLE 2: COACHING SCENARIOS AND BUSINESS VALUE

Development Area	Description	Key Business Value	ROI
Performance in current role	• Functioning in current role • Clarify performance goals and needs of role • Assessment and action planning • Potentially address derailers and blind spots	• Improve executive performance • Avert turnover • Diminish team disengagement risk	$

Development Area	Description	Key Business Value	ROI
Future development preparation	• For pipeline/succession needs of organization • Prepare for leap in scope or responsibility • Learn new leadership approaches (and unlearn others) needed at higher levels	• Deepen succession bench • Ensure readiness for leaps in scope • Broaden skills of high potentials	$
Executive agenda	• Ongoing insight and perspective • Thought partner and sounding board on decisions • Useful during dramatic change	• Enhance decision-making • Improve strategic thinking • Lead change effectively	$
Specific skill development	• Specific skills for current role • On the job, supplemented with classroom or with instructors	• Grow in key leadership skills (see below)	$
Assimilation / On-boarding	• Quickly become productive in new role or company • Learn culture • Establish key relationships • Find quick wins • Make decisions on team, strategy, etc.	• Accelerate ramp-up • Diminish turnover risk of new execs • Increase organizational credibility	$

The ROI column is where things get interesting, and you're right to wonder about what numbers go in that column. If coaching makes you a more effective leader, what ROI can you expect?

The rationale for any coaching engagement should include a discussion of the return to the organization. Some leading voices and practitioners within the coaching profession calculate ROI for coaching engagements using a standard equation such as this:

Chapter Four – What Is the ROI of Coaching?

$$\text{ROI} = \frac{\text{Cost of coaching}}{\text{Profit improvement attributable to coaching}}$$

The return on investment can come in the form of time savings and efficiency, cost reductions, productivity, revenue growth, margin growth, overall profitability, reduction in turnover, and more. It's not difficult to predict impressive returns. In fact, the ROI reported by coaching clients themselves is typically six to 100 times the coaching investment.

I can't do the ROI math for you. Knowing the specifics of your situation and the gains you expect in key business values, you might find it interesting to calculate ROI.

So I can't do the math for you. I also WON'T do it for my own coaching gigs.

What makes me say that? Simple—the math just doesn't go far enough.

A hard-nosed PWC study reported a range of coaching ROI of 10 to 49 times coaching investment. Getting an acceptable financial return, therefore, is a lay-up. In most cases, the cost of coaching for even lower level managers can be quickly recouped.

Don't get me wrong. I don't object to crunching numbers. It's laudable, but I want to hammer the point that your ROI on coaching should go well beyond immediate financial gains. Most of my clients have six-figure or even seven-figure compensation packages. A few hours of improved efficiencies pay back the cost of coaching. And these senior executives frequently make decisions worth millions or tens of millions of dollars. A single incrementally better decision makes the cost vanish into a rounding error.

There's more. Frankly, in many cases, the improvements in costs or revenues aren't solely attributable to coaching. That's just one factor in any individual's development. A dutiful executive who wants to please the coach and justify the cost might self-report that coaching alone caused the improvement. An arrogant coach might claim the same. Ugh.

Sorry—but if ALL you get out of the coaching engagement is a cost or margin improvement, in my mind, the partnership has been less than fully successful. Sure, go ahead and do the ROI calculation. Pat yourself on the back. But move on to a substantive discussion about what ELSE you will get from coaching.

Here's a dirty little secret: Coaches gravitate to this ROI discussion out of self-interest. They want to sell more coaching, and "hard numbers" are part of the sales pitch. Or they're an answer to a price objection from the potential client, a demonstration of the great return they'll get. This kind of stuff keeps coaches busy congratulating themselves for being so business-minded.

I insist the business improvement discussion be broader. More factors. More subjective. Less measurable but still observable. There's a lot to be gained from coaching, as I detailed in the previous chapter. Go ahead and look back at the lists and see for yourself. The growth can be almost priceless. Rather than repeat that discussion, let me suggest further questions to help you discover the real impact of coaching for you:

- When you achieve your goals for coaching, how will your business abilities be different? What visible or behind-the-scenes impact will you create? How will you improve the organization?

- How will your experience of being coached impact others in your orbit? How will it increase the effectiveness of your team?

- What personal improvements do you foresee?

- How will achieving your coaching goals impact customers or your credibility in the marketplace?

- What factors unique to your organization and industry can a coach help you picture and plan for?

- Which of your outcomes can be sharpened to be more tangible or measurable?

Chapter Four – What Is the ROI of Coaching?

Paying for Your Own Coach

A sponsoring organization almost always pays for executive coaching. What if you want coaching yet lack organizational support? Or what if you want help but don't want anyone at work to find out?

Nothing prevents you from pursuing coaching on your own, and many coaches will take you on as a "self-pay" or "retail" client. A few things to consider in these situations:

- How will people in your organization react if you decide to involve others?

- How much benefit will you take away from coaching without ample information, feedback, and support from others? Can silence and secrecy still accomplish your objectives?

- What's your own ROI for the coaching engagement? Your goals will be different than those of the organization, and they probably have as much to do with career and advancement as they do with performance in your current role.

- What potential issues of perception do you need to address? Is your organization particularly cost-conscious? Who might wonder why so much money is being spent on you?

Saying No to Coaching

People are sometimes inclined to say no to coaching.

Not long ago, I worked with the COO of a large company who originally said no to coaching. He didn't want to be psychoanalyzed. He was too busy. He's a no-B.S. type of executive with no time for squishy stuff.

The organization pressed him to partner with me to get feedback and put together an action plan, largely because his initial adaptation to the company's strong, unique culture had been bumpy. People in this super-nice Midwestern company bristled at his directness, and he also had to deal daily with a direct report who had aspired to the COO job.

Although this leader had corrected his problem behaviors, his boss and board wanted to ensure the changes stuck. He willingly accepted my help gathering feedback and designing a plan. He didn't like everything he heard but he began to see himself as others did. We identified a couple of interconnected blind spots and outlined changes that would make the biggest difference for him. As we built trust, the relationship evolved, and he eventually asked if we could continue with a full coaching engagement. He had come to appreciate having a partner and a sounding board. And yes, he liked to vent from time to time. (But only for five minutes per session. Remember my rule?)

Why do people say no to coaching? Generally, they report being too busy.

Everyone is too busy. Some of my clients look like Edvard Munch's painting "The Scream" when I see them. While most executives are very busy, this in itself is rarely sufficient reason to reject coaching.

In fact, a coach can help you prioritize, allocate resources, negotiate internally, and drive your agenda.

If you decide to say no to coaching, do it with your eyes open.

- Understand you're turning down a terrific, perhaps one-time chance.

- Consider what the organization is telling you. They think you're worth investing in. They want you to be part of its future.

- Regardless of whether you're teetering on the edge of an exit or a central part of the team of tomorrow, don't make a knee-jerk decision. Partnering with a coach can be an extraordinary opportunity to up your game and work on points important to you and to others.

Sometimes busyness is just code, and the real reason for declining a coaching opportunity lies buried, perhaps even from your conscious mind, lurking in the Hidden or Unknown quadrants of the Johari window. It often originates from fear—of what you might find, of being vulnerable, of looking stupid, of what others might say if you work with a coach. Is now the time to face your fears? I invite you to ask yourself just one question:

Is there something else going on?

Bob Kegan and Lisa Lahey of Harvard University say most of us have a foot on the gas to move harder and faster, yet all the while, our other foot pumps the brake. The brake is our beliefs that get in the way. We often aren't aware of all our machinations that hold ourselves back. Chapter 11 covers this in more detail.

My suggestion? Pedal to the metal. Foot off the brake. Prepare to be amazed at how fast you'll go!

Why Not DIY?

Some people prefer to coach themselves. Continuous improvement is laudable. At the start of the next chapter, I'll tell you about a CEO, a leader who exemplifies that trait more than anyone I've ever met. But the stuff of coaching can be a difficult DIY project:

- It's easy to fool yourself about what holds you back.

- It's difficult to collect feedback on yourself. People might not be candid. Even when people are honest, you might rationalize, justify, or excuse your behavior. Coaches ensure that feedback is complete and in context, that you hear it, and that you don't dismiss it.

- It's also difficult to put an action plan together. As executives, we often stop at our first good idea. Coaches are repositories of development actions and have a plethora of resources you might not know about to aid in professional growth.

- Accountability can be a challenge for the DIY coach. While most successful executives are highly accountable, this important-but-not-urgent stuff often gets back-burnered. Just like the gym buddy, the coach shows up for the session, prompting you to do your homework.

- Unearthing and getting rid of years' worth of stubborn thought patterns and habits is—well, not easy. But it's attainable with a coach.

Honestly, most executives lack experience understanding and applying the science of human behavior and change. It's hard to cut your own hair!

Know Why

I recently coached an executive from a consumer-packaged-goods company. He sought me out because his HR person had pulled him aside and suggested he work with a coach. The HR person was carrying a message from management, as often happens, but the message went unsaid until he asked.

The executive's first question was *Why?*

Fair question. He wanted to know which category he belonged in. Troubled? High potential? The guy who needs to sharpen an edge or sand off a corner?

In his case, the organizational *why* was about improving in a couple of areas—communication and executive presence—to ensure he stays effective. The organization hopes to retain him in leadership for another decade and wants him to continue growing.

When your organization proposes a coach, don't hesitate to ask *why*. Even before your first steps in the coaching process, get an idea where you're going. Choose to get excited about the destination and what you'll learn on the way.

When you can embrace the full ROI of an intensive coaching engagement, I'm fairly sure you'll see its value. In the next chapter, we'll explore your readiness for coaching.

CHAPTER FOUR—KEY QUESTIONS

- Why does your organization want you to engage with a coach?

- Do you disagree with any of your organization's goals for your development? On what points? Are your hesitations significant enough to derail your coaching engagement?

- Who in your organization will judge the ROI of this investment? What metrics will they use?

- What observable, measurable outcomes will show your success?

- When would coaching be so important to you that you would pay out of your own pocket?

- Should you say no to coaching? Why?

CHAPTER FIVE

Are You Ready for Coaching?

You gotta wanna.

– My Dad

A leading high technology CEO once delighted me with a description of what he learned from his years as a brash up-and-comer and his subsequent promotion to president of a key company division while still in his 30s.

Early in his tenure, he received some tough feedback from his team.

The new president thought he was hot stuff.

His people said he was ice cold.

The new president took days to process these difficult messages.

In the past, he might have defended his behavior, believing that turning up the heat was what it took to motivate people and move fast. But now, he didn't try to justify his actions. Or even explain his intentions. He did more than accept the feedback. He embraced it. He set out to change, newly aware that his behavior could impede his work, damage his reputation, and stymie his ambitions.

Today, in the capstone role of his career, this leader still seeks to improve himself daily as he directs a large and incredibly complex organization in a volatile, uncertain, complex, and ambiguous world. He reads voraciously. He dialogs with people throughout the company. He invites feedback from every direction. He triangulates to get as many perspectives as he can. He remains open to new points of view. He realizes that he never knows enough, agreeing that, as *New York Times* writer Thomas Friedman and many others have said, the rate of change in the world is accelerating, and standing still is falling behind.

What makes this CEO exceptional isn't his intellect, though he is unusually smart. It isn't his people leadership, though he's great at that as well. And it isn't his business acumen, presence, charisma, or temperament, though those are all towering strengths.

The CEO possesses those rare qualities in part because relatively early in his career, he seized an opportunity to reorient and move in a direction that ensured his ongoing success. Simply put, he chooses to take steps to get better every day. Complacency makes him uneasy. He leads others graciously, but he never says "good enough" when it comes to his own development.

This executive's drive and desire is now more than matched by tremendous empathy, compassion, and caring. This powerful combination has turbocharged him as an executive and as a human being, making him a world-class CEO and wonderful leader.

Opportunity Meets Openness

To maximize your growth as an executive, two factors are indispensable. Either is powerful on its own, but the combination of these factors potentiates the other, making a coaching engagement exponentially more impactful.

Factor one is **opportunity**. You notice a gap to fill. The opportunity might be a personal need for growth or an organizational need for greater strength. Or it may be a combination of personal and organizational necessities.

Factor two is **openness**. As demonstrated by the CEO above, openness isn't passive. It's a vital activity. Receptivity. Willingness. Being okay being wrong. Desire to learn. Craving to try new things. Doing the hard work. Pushing through discomfort. And eventually, building new strength.

Identifying Opportunites

So let's get practical, granular, and immediately relevant. Below I list opportunities where executive coaching is particularly useful, sorted into personal developmental needs and organizational situations. Your task is to determine which area is most pertinent for you right now. The list isn't exhaustive, so I left space at the bottom to add your own growth areas.

Work through these lists, marking in the right-hand column whether for you that opportunity is HIGH, MEDIUM, or LOW. You'll get a picture of the areas you want to focus on in your coaching engagement.

Personal Developmental Needs	Opportunity		
Enhance leadership capabilities—leading through others, delegation, executive presence, decision-making	H	M	L
Executive temperament—addressing issues of balance, toughness (too much/not enough), confidence, perseverance, dealing with ambiguity, empathy, excessive caution, volatility	H	M	L
Develop a new skill—gaining expertise for your current or future roles, such as financial acumen, presentation skills, strategic planning	H	M	L
Derailers or blind spots—addressing traits including abrasiveness, timidity, reactivity, insensitivity, cynicism, low trust, shading the truth, impulsiveness, being disorganized, or not prioritizing	H	M	L
Bad behavior when triggered—curtailing impulses to fight, flight, freeze, appease; shooting the messenger, angry outbursts, running for cover	H	M	L
Ambition to grow or move up—creating a plan to move up a level or more, gaining ability to lead leaders	H	M	L
Relationship finesse—increasing EQ* demonstrated in handling tricky situations with tact, effectively navigating organizational politics, negotiating internally, exercising influence, leading people in the organizational matrix who don't report to you	H	M	L
Managing stress—overcoming challenges, building resilience, sustaining a fast pace to keep up with the organization, developing effectiveness and thriving in all aspects of life	H	M	L
Other			
	H	M	L
	H	M	L
	H	M	L

---

* Daniel Goleman has demonstrated successful executives are distinguished not by IQ but EQ (emotional intelligence). While intellect is the price of admission to the executive suite, rarely do senior leaders vary much in IQ. Success at this level comes from the ability get things done through and with people.

Organizational Situations	Opportunity		
New company or new role—getting a jump start and avoiding the high failure rate of newly hired executives; dealing with watch-outs in new roles, like managing former peers	H	M	L
Leading dramatic change—mastering the ability to lead transformational change through major events like mergers, acquisitions, restructurings, realignments, cultural or industry upheavals	H	M	L
Leadership changes—thriving under a new manager or a new executive in your function or company, managing rapid change or shifts in priorities	H	M	L
Difficult boss—dealing with all aspects of the most critical relationship in anyone's work life, filtering feedback, managing up, building collaboration	H	M	L
Successful preparation—discerning developmental needs, knowing "what got you here won't get you there," gaining domain experience, leadership capability	H	M	L
Start-ups—leading anything new, such as a new function, business, or company; enhancing skills in focus, organizing, structuring, and prioritizing	H	M	L
Handling hardships—difficult assignments, travel, long hours, business transitions, organizational decline	H	M	-
Big picture—creating vision, determining strategy, changing culture, communicating effectively	H	M	L
Other			
	H	M	L
	H	M	L
	H	M	L

Working through this exercise helps you begin to identify opportunities for growth. A coach will further help you define and refine your needs. Many clients want additional focus in advance of the coaching engagement. To better define your opportunities, consider these options:

- ask current and former peers
- ask current and former managers
- ask former direct reports
- review assessments and 360s
- review performance appraisals and other feedback

These data points will clarify your needs and highlight your most significant growth opportunities. The effort might even give you energy to get started.

Assessing Openness

Identifying your prime development opportunities is just the first of two factors that maximize your potential for exponential growth. The second thing you can do? Assess and increase your openness.

Maybe you're already all-in, eager to get rolling with your coaching engagement. If so, I still encourage you to read the next few paragraphs. And if you're not good to go, this section will be particularly helpful.

I've learned the hard way that not everyone is ready for the opportunity presented by coaching. But no matter how you got here, what happens next matters far more.

When I meet with prospective clients to discuss the coaching process, a conversation I call a "chemistry meeting," the executive almost always has a stack of questions to get answered about the process and about me.

For my part, I have only one question in mind:

Is this person open to coaching?

If the answer is no, I decline the engagement.

Early in my coaching career, I struggled with two clients who clearly weren't open to coaching. I took them on because I liked their bosses or their companies and wanted to help.

I failed at both assignments. Miserably. Really.

Maybe a better coach could have brought them around. That's certainly what I hoped when I started, but over many months and meetings, little happened except we wasted time and money. Both engagements ended by mutual consent.

It took two turns on that adventure ride for me to learn my lesson.

I'm an optimist. And a slow learner.

I discovered, for example, that the threat of losing a job doesn't make anyone more receptive to coaching. It might even diminish their ability to try. People who feel threatened fall into the flight-fight-freeze-appease mode we humans adopted when we were being chased by sabre-tooth tigers and giant prehistoric rodents. People in frightening situations display a laser focus, coupled with cognitive and biochemical obstacles that inhibit learning ANYTHING. All their blood is diverted to their legs and rapidly pumping hearts. The oxygen-starved brain barks just one instruction: "RUN!"

I've learned to hold out hope for these situations, but I've observed that progress generally comes through methodical performance improvement plans, stringent standards, and close monitoring and correction. Here's why: The executive facing a PIP (Performance Improvement Plan) must comply. In contrast, an executive should enter coaching of their own volition with at least the spark of a desire to learn, improve, and grow. The more openness and willingness to try something new, the better.

Let me put my big question to you:

How open are you to coaching?

My Coaching Readiness Curve below lets you explore that question and helps you assess how receptive you are to partnering with a coach.

1. Study the scale and read the definitions of several stops along the way from "closed" to "open." Decide where you place yourself. Write "ME" to mark your spot.

2. Assess where others would place you. Note that we often grade ourselves higher than we should, or we aren't aware of blind spots. Jot a name or two or more to mark those spots.

3. Consider this question: What would it take to move you toward the "open" end of the scale? Write your answer somewhere you won't lose it, like in the margin of this page. There are also a few tips below to give you some ideas.

COACHING READINESS CURVE

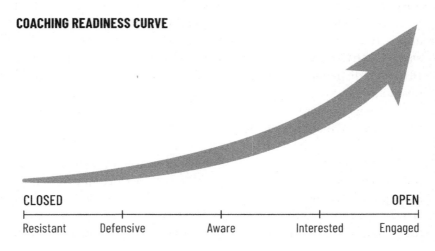

CLOSED				OPEN
Resistant	Defensive	Aware	Interested	Engaged

Engaged	**I'm all in.** Whatever it takes, I want to do it. I expect some challenges, but life will be worse if I don't.
Interested	**I'm curious.** I probably can learn a lot and that appeals to me. I might be uncomfortable at times. That unnerves me a bit.
Aware	**I have issues.** But is this really the best use of my time? What if I refuse to do it? I'd better find out more. Maybe I can get better.
Defensive	**Whoa! Really?** Who put that feedback in my coffee? That's crazy. I'm not like that. But I don't want to totally shut the door either. I'll take one more step to see.
Resistant	**What a load of crap!** Who has time? My boss is a jerk. I've got better things to do. I don't need a shrink. What I need is for you to get moving, on the double!

If your honest assessment is that you're living in the Resistant zone, you might think things like "This is a waste of time" or "I'm only here because my boss says I have to be" or "What a bunch of B.S.!" or "I'm just checking the box."

I would advise you not to embark on coaching.

You're not ready.

Yet.

Give it a few days and see if you can reconsider, like the CEO at the start of this chapter. He got tough feedback, resisted it at first, but eventually used it as a catalyst for ongoing improvement that just won't stop. He's now hard-wired to get better and better.

Last chapter, I mentioned the COO who at first wasn't interested in coaching. Are you prepared for a surprise? Like him, most of my clients or prospective clients land somewhere in the middle of the readiness scale. Few are completely resistant, only a handful are wildly enthusiastic.

So don't fret. I know you're busy, skeptical, questioning, and concerned. The issue is how you can move up the Readiness Curve. Heading in that direction means you're more receptive, more energetic, more willing to try new things. You'll make the coaching experience a priority. And you're far more likely to make significant progress.

You Gotta Wanna

I invite you to be open, curious, and willing to use executive coaching as a catalyst to be a stronger leader. Without openness, coaching goes nowhere. You get out of it what you put into it, like anything else. As my dad always says about winning at anything big, "You gotta wanna!"

Still not feeling it? I've learned a few tricks to get more engaged in almost anything, including executive coaching. Try just one or two of these and see if you don't feel more enthused about working and winning with a coach.

- **Be here now.** Be present. Just enjoy the moment. Appreciate the opportunity. Get what you can from each interaction.

- **Ask questions and get curious.** Seek to understand yourself, others, how things work, how to increase your effectiveness. Curiosity moves people from a negative to neutral to positive frame of mind.

- **Commit before you're ready.** Shall I tell you how I decided to marry my wife of nearly four decades? I asked her. The commitment came after. I said yes, then figured it out as I went along.

- **Put it near the top of your list**. Move it to the top five, the things you think about and work on every day. Just putting it there will draw your focus and attention.

- **Ask what you can get out of it**. Yes, self-focus and self-interest. What's in it for me? If you assess this opportunity honestly, you'll come to believe that you can seize the moment for a big leap in capability.

- **Think how much it will mean to others.** Ponder the people who matter most to you—at work, at home, in the community. Think how much it will mean to them to have a NEW AND IMPROVED YOU. Think how wowed they'll be to see you change. They'll think you're changing for them and love and appreciate you all the more.

- **Change the equation.** Anticipation of discomfort might be the heart of your reluctance. I'd suggest that climbing out of your comfort zone is what it takes to learn something new. In most parts of life, the equation becomes DISCOMFORT = IMPROVEMENT.

In these initial chapters, we've covered a lot of ground. But the adventure is just beginning. You know what coaching is, what it does, and what you'll get out of it. You have a solid idea of what you want to work on.

In the next chapters, I'll let you in on the coaching process, plus how to select a coach, get feedback, create a change plan, and sustain momentum. The tips and revelations will help you own the coaching sequence from end to end. Not only will you be an educated buyer, but you'll learn how to customize the product to meet your unique needs.

CHAPTER FIVE—KEY QUESTIONS

- What are your top personal development needs?

- What organizational situations could you address in executive coaching?

- How open are you to coaching? Where are you on the Readiness Curve?

- What holds you back from enthusiastically engaging in a coaching opportunity?

- Do you "wanna"? What can you do to move toward "I'm all in"?

- When others ask what you hope to gain through this opportunity, what will you say?

PART TWO

PART TWO

CHAPTER SIX

Master the Coaching Process

> *If you don't know where you're going,
> you'll end up someplace else.*
>
> – Yogi Berra

I was at the start of a chemistry meeting with an emerging technology leader at one of the nation's biggest banks. We had barely started when he interrupted with a query I hear from virtually every prospective client: "Can you tell me about your coaching process?"

Great question.

If I didn't answer quickly, he'd soon be fidgeting with his smart phone.

I'll tell you what I told him, so you can master the coaching process and thereby control your destiny. If you grasp what coaches do, the key methods they employ, and the structure of a typical coaching session, that knowledge is power. You'll steer the coaching engagement to make it more efficient and effective for you, and you'll prepare for individual sessions in a way that maximizes your takeaway.

So here goes—my five-step process:

Step one	Clarify initial coaching outcomes desired by the client and organization
Step two	Assess strengths and weaknesses using tools customized to the engagement
Step three	Design a developmental action plan based on the assessments and organizational expectations
Step four	Coach to the plan, motivating the client to test new behaviors and do the hard work that achieves results
Step five	Build a plan for when coaching ends, so the client sustains new learnings

That five-step process moves a client from initiation of coaching to integration of learning into their career.

These steps, by the way, assume contracting and other logistics are complete. I'll address those details in Chapter eight.

Other coaches describe their process with different terms or vary the steps slightly, but few veer wildly from this approach.

Adapting the Five Steps

Although I just spelled out five steps, no coaching relationship ever duplicates another. So I tailor the five steps to each situation. For example, clients have sometimes taken assessments during the selection process or an internal leadership program. Some have been assessed to death. In each instance, we incorporate existing information into the coaching process. I don't have clients repeat assessments completed within the last couple of years; though, depending on the situation, I may add another tool or two to gain additional data.

Likewise, some clients arrive with a development plan. Rather than reinvent that document, we use it as a starting point and revise based on what we discover in the first two steps. The result might be a wholesale replacement, a rewrite, or a tweak.

Finally, there are situations where this process seems to make less sense, like when a client just wants a sounding board or if a developmental need is spoken from on high and the coach is contracted to focus on, for example, presentation skills. However, even when it seems smart to move directly from clarifying outcomes to forming an action plan, I almost always encourage some kind of assessment. It's dangerous to make assumptions without verifying them, and this discovery step might expose other needs that take precedence.

With those caveats in mind, let's examine each step. After that, we'll look at the coaching session itself and the techniques coaches employ to drive results.

More About the Five Steps

EXECUTIVE COACHING PROCESS

Clarify Outcomes	Assess	Develop Plan	Try and Test	Sustain
• Agree on expectations • Interview client and stakeholders • Review organizational strategy, priorities, and objectives • Develop initial outcomes and action plan • Commence coaching	• Administer and interpret assessments • 360 interviews • Review performance data • Discuss feedback with client • Refine action plan	• Finalize coaching outcomes with all stakeholders • Develop action steps to drive development • Continue habit of regular coaching meetings • Gain client buy-in to plan and build enthusiasm	• Coach to the plan • Motivate the client to test new behaviors • Gather feedback from allies • Solicit insights from key stakeholders • Hold the client accountable for progress	• Reflect on progress • Determine next growth steps • Build sustainability plan • Conduct closure meeting with stakeholders to evaluate and celebrate success

STEP ONE: Clarify Outcomes

Clarifying outcomes at the start requires only a meeting or two, and it's easy to shortcut this step. Yet it addresses important objectives:

- The coach and client get acquainted and establish a relationship of mutual trust and clear expectations.

- The coach becomes familiar with the organization as well as the client's role, priorities, and challenges.

- The coach and client draft outcomes and preliminary coaching plan.

- The coach verifies alignment on outcomes with client and boss.

- The coach and client address logistics like scheduling meetings and assessments.

I always meet with the client and manager—often together, sometimes not—to discuss desired outcomes. Briefings with the boss or HR or the chemistry meeting with the client all touch on outcomes, all-important conversations that frame the rest of the process. These forthright discussions ensure boss and client are aligned on the reasons for coaching.

During the intake, I ask the following outcome-focused questions. You can answer these questions for yourself right now:

- Why did you decide to engage in coaching?

- What do you hope to accomplish?

- What are your top three to five goals for coaching?

- What benefits will you get from coaching?

- What benefits will your organization get?

- What obstacles might you encounter?

- What does success look like?

As we identify outcomes at this early stage, I try to keep them high level, more "enhance leadership effectiveness" than "delegate better." Although I want to know what leadership effectiveness looks like to the client and boss, the client and I reserve the right to further define needs based on upcoming assessments and data gathering.

STEP TWO: Assess

With the client completing assessments as the coach conducts interviews and gathers 360 feedback, this phase of gathering, analyzing, and digesting data can take up to a couple of months.

I devote a full chapter (nine) to assessments, so I won't duplicate that material here.

This step is where you receive one of two great gifts a coach can give—greater internal and external self-awareness, which I discussed earlier.

Assessments delve into the values, beliefs, and thoughts that drive your behavior. And they uncover how others view you. The result? You discover blind spots. You acquire a deeper understanding of your strengths and weaknesses. What you learn prepares you for step three, creating a development plan.

The weeks of assessments and debrief are perfect for coaching meetings focused on issues raised in the first step or on timely work concerns.

STEP THREE: Develop a Plan

After gaining understanding of your strengths and growth areas, it's time to create a development plan. Again, I devote Chapter eight to this important topic.

The development plan isn't a document you create and shelve to never touch again. It's all about action. It's the most important document to come from the coaching process. Frankly, I hate paperwork, so often it's the only document.

Writing what you want to work on and committing to specific action is essential to the dramatic gains executives look for. This document helps you focus, prioritize, and track progress. Should you choose to share the plan with others, your allies can use it to checklist your accountabilities. Typically, the coach, client, and boss hold a three-way meeting to review the plan, gain alignment on goals and actions, and enlist support wherever needed.

STEP FOUR: Try and Test New Behaviors

New behaviors. Testing. Results. Wins. Losses. Regrouping. Retrying. Success!

After you finalize the development plan, you act. *What happens when I try THAT... it didn't work as expected... I need to attempt something else.* Or *I had great success... I'll do more of that and see what additional gains I get.*

Here's where you'll spend the bulk of your coaching experience—or should we call it what it is, an ongoing experiment, a laboratory for success at work. Since progress in this phase is self-reported, many clients ask me to touch base with key stakeholders. I often reach out to the same people I contacted during the assessment phase to get their perspective on how it's going.

Coaching guru Marshall Goldsmith's idea of the mini-360 is useful. In just 15 minutes per conversation, I can ask the boss, direct reports, and other colleagues a few simple questions, tabulate results, and serve up fresh feedback to the client. I summarize everything so individual responses can't be identified, protecting anonymity and ensuring candor.

Check the appendix at the back of the book for the questions I ask in my version of the mini-360.

STEP FIVE: Sustain

Once upon a time, I employed a four-step process. Now I know that a fifth step, a plan for sticky learning, is critical. I reserve two final sessions to consolidate learning and sketch out a plan for what comes next after the formal coaching engagement concludes. We're shooting for sustainability. What will it take to keep up the momentum? Chapter 12 describes this critical step and gives you a template for ongoing growth.

The Coaching Session: What to Expect

Early in my coaching career, a client said she was nervous prior to the first coaching session. She wasn't sure how she should prepare or how things would go.

I've since found that most of my clients are anxious before that initial meeting. Beneath the bravado, poise, and practiced executive presence, they're a little raw. At first it surprised me, but I began to understand as I gained more experience.

Leaders lead. Executives command and control. And talking with a coach is like visiting a doctor who glances at the results of routine blood work and says, almost under her breath, "Hmmm... let's order some more tests and see what's going on." Nothing is worse than wondering what might unfold or fearing a loss of control. When a coach shows up, the client's underlying feeling might be *I'm putting myself and my career in this coach's hands. I hope it's safe. I hope I do it right.*

Coaching sessions can go any direction. The utter unpredictability—I love it—messy human beings muddling forward together. Sometimes we work on process steps, run through assessment data, create the development plan, or brainstorm options for new behaviors. Other times, we play with live ammo—whatever topics, issues, or challenges the executive wants to address.

Coaching sessions are normally scheduled every two to three weeks. Any shorter and not enough has happened to merit a discussion. Any longer and we spend most of the meeting just catching up and there isn't enough time to get down to business.

To prepare for each coaching meeting, I suggest my clients ask themselves a few questions and jot answers in a log or journal where they also keep other notes, learnings, etc.

I have a major conviction behind my urging prework. I want executives to feel they own the session and take final responsibility for what happens. It's MY job to facilitate them doing THEIR job. This approach is completely opposite what clients usually expect, so I set this expectation up front.

Given that you own the coaching process, you'll get far more out of meetings if you take five minutes the day before the session to consider these questions:

COACHING SESSION PREPARATION QUESTIONS

Check-in	How am I doing overall?
Follow-up	What do we need to follow up from the last coaching session?
Report	What action(s) did I undertake since our last session? What were my wins? Losses? What did I learn from my homework?
Goalsetting	What do I want to get out of today's coaching session?
Exploration	What additional issues, challenges, concerns, achievements, or areas of learning should we address?

By the way, after I answered the question on process from the prospective technology client, this was his follow-up: "What happens if something comes up that isn't related to what we are working on right then?"

"Well," I said. "You're out of luck. We have to stay on task."

Not really.

I answered that the process flexes. Coaching starts day one, meaning that if the client brings an issue, topic, or opportunity to explore or address, most of the time, that's what we do. For the client, this often forms the most valuable part of the coaching experience, even more than the formal process.

Occasionally, I challenge a client who wants to deviate from plan because I suspect they're avoiding a problematic area. Still, it's always the client's decision how we use our time. My role is to remind the client of the process, where we're at, and what remains to be done.

Your coach will have a process that guides each session, though it may remain in the background, unspoken. Most executive coaches have been taught something like the GROW model for structuring a coaching session. They use this problem-solving process to help clients resolve issues or address challenges and opportunities. It's a simple model I never let my clients get away without learning. I want them equipped with a tool to coach themselves when they don't know what to do next.

COACHING GROW MODEL

Stage	Coach's Role	Steps
Goal	Clarify the goal	• Help the client set clear goals • Agree on central challenge or focus for today's discussion
Reality	Gain insight	• Clarify situation • Invite self-assessment • Determine impact • Determine future implications • Provide observations/feedback

Options	Generate options	• Brainstorm options • Assess pros and cons • Coach offers options only if needed
Way Forward	Commit to best actions	• Select best options • Identify potential obstacles • Determine needed support

Top coaching techniques

Coaches deploy innumerable techniques during a session and over an engagement. These methods invite clients to shift perspective, gain new insight, acquire a skill, enhance empathy, understand the need for action, better regulate, and so on.

Some techniques float above the waterline. Others run silent in the deep. My approach is to speak overtly with clients about what I'm doing without overwhelming or distracting them from the task at hand. I disclose the technique I'm using if it will help in the moment or fill a future need. When I do disclose, I might ask ahead of time, "Would you be open to trying something...." Or I explain after the fact, "You may have noticed that I tried...."

There are too many techniques to elaborate here. Each coach chooses techniques based on client needs, unique circumstances, and the coach's training and personal preferences. I'll highlight a few high-leverage techniques because they're commonly used, extraordinarily effective, and work magic at home—but please practice them on yourself first! Equipping yourself with these top techniques will also help you self-sustain and expand your growth after your work with a coach wraps up.

TOP TECHNIQUE ONE: Powerful Questions

We all think we ask good questions. That's what executives do. They dive deep to understand. They prod and poke. They challenge thinking. All the while, they build their own knowledge base.

Powerful coaching questions are different. They're questions NO ONE knows the answers to. At least not at first. They force you to ponder, make you explore, and lead you to your own understanding and insights.

People think coaching is about giving advice, and indeed, all executive coaching professionals (and pretenders) must ward off that temptation. But doling out wisdom is most emphatically not what good coaches do. Giving advice usually tanks:

- The recommendations might not suit the client.

- Someone else's notion of what to do rarely gets unreserved buy-in.

- Getting advice doesn't increase client capabilities.

By contrast, good questions empower. They help the client discover solutions and build new pathways and skills.

Consider these key characteristics of good questions. (I'm belaboring this point because good inquiry is a potent skill for executives, not just for coaches.)

- **Good questions are OPEN-ENDED.** They can't be answered with a simple YES or NO.

    - Closed-ended: Can you realistically take that on too?

    - Open-ended: How would things change if you take that on too?

- **Good questions are BROAD.** There's no embedded solution. They don't lead. They don't reveal a "correct" answer.

- Narrow: Don't you need to check that out with your boss?

- Broad: Who do you need to check this out with?

- **Good questions STAND ALONE.** I could give you an example of this, but I would embarrass myself. Stacking questions is my biggest flaw, rattling off multiple follow-ups to clarify my original question. The fix? Ask one question at a time. And then, as uncomfortable as it may be, **stay silent** while the other person thinks.

Here are my top ten coaching questions. You can employ them in all kinds of situations, not just coaching, which is one reason I like them:

And what else? Tell me more.	The **probing** question
What's the central challenge here for you?	The **focus** question
What do you want?	The **outcomes** question
If you say yes to this, what will you say no to?	The **prioritizing** question
If you do this, how will things look different?	The **visioning** question
What are your options? How will you evaluate them?	The **brainstorming** question
If you were the other person, what would you want?	The **empathy** question
What is your part in creating this situation?	The **accountability** question
How would you like this to move forward?	The **proactivity** question
What were the key takeaways for you from this?	The **learning** question

Note how many of these great questions start with WHAT or HOW. That start usually works better than WHEN, WHERE, WHO, or WHY. WHY questions can work but often elicit known information rather than foster growth through questioning.

TOP TECHNIQUE TWO: Reframing

I learned this technique from my daughter, a licensed clinical social worker. We easily get mired in our own points of view. Often, those viewpoints run in our brains on a continuous loop and we can't find our way out.

Questioning our assumptions in situations where our views, values, beliefs, or thoughts have us stuck in a thinking rut can break us free.

We can go directly after our assumptions, doing our best to identify them. We often find they're based on incomplete or inaccurate data.

Cue my "grumpy boss story," an illustration that quickly explains everything you need to know about reframing.

I met my boss in the hall one morning and greeted him with a cheery "Hello!" He not only didn't respond, but he looked away and gave me a sour frown.

I thought I was in deep trouble for sure. For the rest of the day, I combed my memory for what I might have done to cause his reaction. I ruminated all night. I lost sleep and woke up worried.

Fortunately, I enjoyed a good relationship with my boss. The next day I asked him what egregious mistake I had committed.

He had no idea what I was talking about. When I brought up his reaction to my greeting, he thought for a moment. Then he said that his wife had called yesterday. She had been in a car accident. She was okay but the car was totaled. That's what my boss was reacting to. He hadn't really seen me in the hallway.

When you reframe, start by rechecking the facts and data that caused you to reach your conclusion.

Try these effective reframing questions:

- What are other possible explanations?
- What are other ways to see it?

TOP TECHNIQUE THREE: Visualization

We know about visualization largely from sports, where our heroes close their eyes before a move to see it in their mind's eye. Much leading-edge athletic training includes visualization of how competition and winning looks and feels.

Visualization uses imagery to prepare yourself to perform. Picture yourself presenting to a large group or providing a high-pressure update to the board of directors. You need peak functioning.

Visualization hasn't helped my golf game. But I'm a believer that it boosts confidence and focus, and there's evidence of better performance. The cause? Body and mind seem to respond similarly to actual and imagined events.

Imagine a successful performance. In effective visualization, you

- **Engage all your senses.** You don't just see yourself making the right moves. You bring the experience alive by involving your mind, body, and senses.
- **Take center stage.** You're not an observer in the audience. You're the star.
- **Practice regularly.** When you can picture detail in your imagery, rehearse it consistently.

In the realm of coaching, it helps to visualize

- a new behavior playing out perfectly
- a future full of the satisfaction of a goal attained

- a positive view of your past and present, picturing what contributes to your future success

TOP TECHNIQUE FOUR: Reflection

You're too damned busy to reflect, right? That's what I hear when I suggest clients use reflection as a tool in the coaching process. Or their eyes glaze over but they say nothing. I can see them flipping a mental calendar of when they'll squeeze THAT in!

Despite our crazed schedules that often preclude us from reflecting, learning and change never happen apart from a lot of wondering and pondering and even a little brooding. We need to step back to evaluate what works or doesn't. We need to pause and see the forests or trees that otherwise escape our notice. We need to review our thoughts and consider how others view the same situations.

David Petersen at Google has come up with a brilliant reflection tactic. Many of my clients love this simple discipline. During your daily commute home, spend three to five minutes quizzing yourself. This repeated, purposeful, focused thought exercise truly takes just minutes, but it brings powerful insights. Try these daily reflection questions:

- What went well today?
- What didn't go well today?
- What new thing did I try?
- What will I do differently tomorrow?

That's it. Simple, easy, fast, and effective.

Look for a weekly and monthly reflection calendar in the appendix.

POWER MOVE

Try the daily reflection questions for a week.

Then reflect: What insights do you gain? How do they improve your effectiveness?

To go deeper, refer to the appendix for the full calendar.

CHAPTER SEVEN

Select the Right Coach

> *Do not hire a man who does your work for money, but him who does it for the love of it.*
>
> – Henry David Thoreau

Jenny's assistant escorted me to a sleek office 30 stories above the streets of downtown Minneapolis. Floor-to-ceiling windows looked down on the Viking's old Metrodome stadium and its inflatable roof, recently collapsed under a foot of snow. She motioned me to a conference table of glass and steel, and I sipped on the gourmet coffee she offered as I waited. I knew Jenny from a professional association, but this was our first business meeting. She was looking for a coach and wanted to connect.

Jenny buzzed with energy as she arrived and set down her folders. After a little catching up, she started with questions about my coaching process. I asked what she wanted to accomplish, then inquired whether she had ever worked with a coach.

"Yes." She paused. "It didn't work out." She looked at her feet. She seemed apologetic. Or embarrassed.

"May I ask what happened?"

"The coach wasn't right for me."

"How so?"

Jenny explained that she chose her coach based on a referral from a higher-level colleague. She trusted the source and didn't want to waste time, so she met with only one coach without investigating other options. The initial meeting was perfunctory, a get-acquainted conversation followed by her quick commitment to engage. Though the coach was well qualified, she concluded after just a few meetings that he wasn't a good fit and cut off the engagement.

The Choice

I ask every potential client that same question: **Have you ever worked with a coach?**

Many say no. Those who indicate yes often relate a story like Jenny's.

Selecting the right coach for you and your circumstances is likely the most important decision you'll make in taking control of the coaching process and ensuring a terrific result.

What you need is a way to explore and evaluate potential choices. Nothing cumbersome, but a method to filter down to the right coaching partner.

I'm not being hyperbolic when I encourage you to treat this decision with the same care you use to choose a physician, therapist, attorney, financial adviser, or to hire a new employee. After all, you're entrusting your executive development to the professional you choose. Making the right choice helps you avoid the consequences of a failed engagement, from lost time and money to potentially deep dents to your reputation. Who gets blamed when coaching falls apart? Maybe you.

I also contend it's harder to pick a coach than a lawyer, doctor, or counselor. Those fields have clear education and certification requirements for entry, along with explicit standards and ethics for ongoing practice. In contrast, anyone can be a coach. There are no universally accepted certification requirements, no set performance standards, no consistent coaching canon, and no consensus on an ethical code that guides the profession.

Nevertheless, there's a straightforward approach you can use to select a highly-qualified coach who fits your situation and style. It's my 3C **Criteria for Coaches:**

- Credentials
- Credible Experience
- Chemistry

The first two criteria, credentials and credible experience, can be evaluated in part by reviewing the coach's website, bio, and LinkedIn profile. For coaches who make the cut of this initial screening, an interview lets you assess chemistry, or interpersonal fit, between you and the coach.

Let me give you the details you need to implement the 3C Criteria.

Credentials

There are no universally accepted credentials for coaches. While many coaches have attended one of the hundreds of coach training programs, not all programs are accredited. And there are multiple accreditation bodies promoting their own varying standards. Some training programs are even accredited by the same group that provides the training! Complicating matters further, many truly excellent coaches have no formal credentials.

You might think about sidestepping that morass by ignoring credentials and looking to experience and chemistry as your primary criteria in selecting a coach. Instead, I suggest that you delve into the training and credentials obtained by coaches on your radar to assess the rigor of their chosen programs. My recommendation is that you review bios and resumes and select only those with coach training credentials for further consideration.

You can refine your assessment of training and credentials during the chemistry interview, asking questions such as:

- What training have you pursued to equip you as a coach?
- Why did you select that program?
- What were the requirements for successfully completing the program?
- What was the program's philosophy (or framework or emphasis)?
- Was the program accredited? By whom?
- Are you certified as a coach? By whom?

By reviewing bios and asking these questions you'll discover that most coaches land in one of three buckets:

1. **The coach has little or no coach-specific training.** I recommend rejecting any coach in this bucket without at least seven years of intensive, credible coaching experience you can independently verify (see next section on experience).

2. **The coach has undertaken less-than-rigorous training.** The credential was awarded after the coach attended a weekend of training. Or the program isn't accredited by an independent body. Or the coach didn't do what it takes to finish an independently accredited program and gain certification. Again, reject coaches in this bucket without at least seven years of verifiable experience.

3. **The coach has completed a rigorous coach-specific training program or holds an advanced degree (Masters or PhD) in a field such as psychology.** If the coach has coach-specific training, ask who accredited the program. If the accreditation

was granted by an independent body like the International Coach Federation (ICF), it's obviously better than approval by the organization delivering the coaching. Many consider the ICF the gold standard in accreditation. It's certainly the largest and most widely recognized.

Many coaches hold degrees in psychology or related social sciences but possess no coach-specific training. Psychologists transition to coaching for a variety of reasons. Some make the move as a natural extension of their work counseling patients or conducting pre-employment assessments. Some do it for their own personal growth. Some want a different type of client. Some don't want to deal with the bureaucracy of insurance. Regardless of the motivation for the career change—which you can explore in the chemistry meeting—many aspects of psychology training transfer to coaching, making an advanced degree (Masters, PhD, or PsyD) in a social science a solid coaching credential.

While I acknowledge that there are coaches with wonderful skills who nevertheless lack formal coaching training, that isn't where the field is going. Meeting the training and certification requirements should be the price of admission for a coach, meaning coaches who lack the training don't get considered for the engagement. This seems harsh and it potentially excludes good coaches, but those who have completed thorough, formal training are more likely to be excellent practitioners, according to research published by David Peterson in 2010. Lack of training is an easy, reliable indicator to help you filter your list of coaches.

Credible Experience

Several varieties of credible experience are relevant to coach selection:

1. Experience overall

2. Experience with people like you—with needs and issues like yours

3. Experience in or with your company or a similar organization

Again, the coach's bio tells you much of what you need to know. Use these questions to go deeper in the chemistry interview:

- Can you tell me about your coaching experience? How many years? How many clients?
- Can you give me examples of your experience coaching people like me?
- When have you worked in organizations like ours?
- What other experience do you have that will contribute to the success of our engagement?

There are no precise thresholds for evaluating experience, but my rule of thumb is that you should choose someone with at least three years of coaching experience with at least 40 clients. Beyond that, it's important that the coach has worked with people at your level and with similar needs. It's optimal if the coach has worked as an employee in a similar organization. Coaches who have sat in your chair are more likely to grasp the demands you face and will better adapt the coaching program to your needs.

The credible experience questions above are relevant even for highly-degreed psychologists and other social science professionals. You'll want to assess their background carefully, weighing their relevant executive coaching experience, not just their history of counseling patients or assessing for selection or promotion. You can also ask how much of their work time they spend coaching vs. counseling, conducting assessments, or other functions. If a psychologist focuses primarily on work outside of coaching, factor that into your decision-making.

Chemistry

The first two criteria, credentials and credible experience, are pass-fail tests. Only if the coach passes these tests do you need to evaluate for personal fit.

Chemistry is more nebulous than credentials or credibility. It involves assessing the style and approach you want, then determining how the coach meshes with your self-assessment.

That's tough to do apart from an interview.

I've found that many executives are uncomfortable interviewing others, especially people like coaches or human resources experts. They presume the interviewee knows far more about interviewing than they do, and as a result, they ask softball questions or dominate the conversation.

Evaluating chemistry with a coach might seem like a purely intuitive task, but there are specific questions you can use to elicit the data you need to assess fit. I've listed these questions below, along with responses to look for from the coach.

Budget an hour for a typical chemistry meeting. You probably won't have time to ask every question, so start with those most pertinent to your concerns:

1. What is your coaching philosophy and approach?

    Look for:

    — Client-focused

    — Belief that the client is resourceful and whole, not helpless or broken

    — Partnership

    — Approach to change

2. What is your coaching process with a new client?

    — Clear, logical process

    — Flexibility

3. What distinguishes you as a coach?

    — Experience and education

    — Approach

4. How will you provide feedback to me? Can you tell me about a time when you've had to give difficult feedback?

    — Employs formal assessments

    — Uses observational or informal feedback

    — Displays courage

5. What assessments will you use?

    — Menu based on specific engagement

    — Self-assessments

    — Feedback from others (360 and/or interviews)

6. What tools and techniques do you use?

    — Variety of approaches

    — Nothing too weird

7. What have clients told you about your approach?

    — What has the coach heard? Does he or she seem self-aware?

    — Willingness to provide references

8. What are you working to improve on as a coach?

    — Self-awareness

- Continuous learner

9. How will you involve my boss? Others? What sort of progress reports do you give them?

    - Frequency and content of reports

    - Client involvement in reviewing reports (for example, in a three-way meeting)

    - Handling confidential information/data (see next question)

10. How do you handle confidentiality?

    - Appreciates need for trust

    - Discussions and data are confidential

    - Sets confidentiality standards up front with all stakeholders

    - Discloses circumstances under which information will be disclosed (such as violation of law or company policy)

11. Can you tell me about one or two of your most successful coaching engagements?

    - Enthusiasm

    - Outcomes tied to role and business that are concrete, positive, sustained

12. What about a very challenging coaching engagement?

    - What this coach struggles with

13. What about a coaching engagement that failed?

    - Honest assessment and understanding

- Mutual responsibility

14. Have you ever refused a coaching engagement? Why?

    - What won't the coach take on and why?

15. How do you ensure learnings and changes carry on beyond the end of the coaching relationship?

    - Ongoing development plan

    - Periodic check-ins

    - Ability to extend engagement and how often this occurs

16. What questions do you have for me?

In an hour chemistry meeting, you should get your most significant questions answered and a strong sense for fit.

I suggest interviewing at least two to three coaches who meet your requirements for education and experience, so you can compare and contrast them. If you interview three potential coaches and still don't feel a fit, keep interviewing until you find one you like. That doesn't mean a coach who agrees with you or is like you. It's often helpful to find someone unlike you and willing to challenge you.

By the way, question number 16 is magic. Asking "What questions do you have for me?" unearths as much as the others combined. I strongly suggest you ask this question in all sorts of interviews, because it elicits the mindset of the person you're interviewing and displays the homework done in preparation—or the lack of it.

Here are a few questions a coach might ask you:

- Why are you interested in coaching?

- Have you worked with a coach before? What did you like? Not like? What did you get out of it?

- What do you want to work on?

- What does success look like in this coaching engagement?

- Have you collected data via a 360 or self-assessment or other tools? What were your key takeaways?

- What do you want in a coach?

- Can you tell me more about your role and your career progression?

- What's your boss's perspective on your development areas? On your need for coaching?

- What have you done so far in your coach selection process?

- What other information can I provide to help you with your decision?

Coaching Philosophies

There's one question I've barely mentioned in this discussion. Sometimes, a prospective client asks me about my coaching philosophy.

I don't have one. Not really.

Some coaches have extensive training in approaches such as Strengths-Based, Appreciative Inquiry, Positive Psychology, Co-Creative, or Presence-Based. They heavily invest in these philosophies and build their coaching process, assessments, and tools around the system.

Other coaches pick and choose among the best of these approaches and apply them as needed.

Most coaching approaches are excellent, with empirical data and experiential practice to back them up.

Some are hokum.

My seatmate on a plane once told me she was a coach. "So am I," I said. She handed me her card. Her coaching philosophy involved crystals and scents, and her card reeked of lavender.

I don't think you need to include coaching philosophy when you choose a coach, which is why I didn't highlight it above. If you find an approach you're really drawn to, fantastic! If so, please make sure it has the other essential elements of the process, and that the coach has the flexibility to use different tools as well.

The fourth C

At the end of the chemistry interview, you could ask the candidate to coach you for ten minutes, to get a sense of approach and style. Invite them to *coach you* on a real but relatively minor challenge you're facing, like an issue with a direct report or a peer, or a challenge with prioritization or communication. You'll instantly get a feel for what it's like to work with this coach.

Keeping pace

An hour isn't much time for your interview, so consider this time budget:

Item	Time
Introductions	2-3 minutes
Credentials questions	5 minutes
Credibility questions	5 minutes

Item	Time
Chemistry questions	30 minutes
Mini-coaching session	10 minutes
Questions from coach	5 minutes
Wrap-up and next steps	2 minutes

When choices are narrowed for you

If you work for a large company, your human resources team might vet coaches, creating a preselected slate of coaches who meet internal standards. Even if these requirements include the 3C Criteria outlined above, it's up to you to ensure your coach meets your own standards and fits your unique situation and personality.

You might be able to answer many of your questions simply by viewing information provided for you, and interviews can primarily focus on chemistry.

Solidify Your Choice

Consider these additional tips as you select your coach:

> **Location.** Large cities have an abundance of coaches and you should be able to identify someone local, unless you need someone highly specialized. If your coach isn't nearby, you'll likely do virtual sessions. Even for local coaches, it's important to clarify that expectation during the chemistry interview.
>
> Many clients prefer face-to-face settings where both sides can pick up on non-verbal communication. Your coach might also want to observe your work environment.

If you're considering working with a coach remotely, do your chemistry interview using the same technology you would use for sessions. I currently have clients in Vienna, Zurich, and Shanghai. I'll meet them in person only once or twice, and we use a variety of voice and video technologies to communicate.

Gender/Identity. Some female executives prefer a male coach because they work in predominantly male environments. Others want a female coach as more relatable. Likewise, a male client might prefer a coach of a specific gender. And some executives might prefer a coach who has the same racial, ethnic, or LGBTQ identity as them. In all of these situations, you want to work with someone you feel comfortable with. The one caution is that you not look for someone like you so you can form a "mutual agreement society" and avoid being challenged.

References. Once you have a finalist, contact a couple of references to see how others describe this coach. Anyone can put on a show for an hour, and a one-hour interview might not reveal what a coaching relationship is really like. When possible, do references with people you know within your company who have worked with the coach. That's your best source of straight information.

Reference checks can be simple 10- or 15-minute conversations. Use these questions when you inquire about a coach:

- When did you work with (coach)?

- What did you like about working with (coach)?

- What did you dislike about working with (coach)?

- Were there any issues that came up in working with (coach)?

- How would you describe (coach)'s style? How did that work for you?

- Did (coach) challenge you?

- How would you assess (coach)'s effectiveness? What would have made him/her more effective?

- Would you recommend (coach)? Why or why not? How strongly?

This quick conversation is more than worth your time.

This process may seem elaborate. But I can't overemphasize its importance. You're choosing a Partner. Capital P. Your Partner at a pivot point in your development. And it's not as complicated as it seems.

During a chemistry meeting with a potential client several months ago, I asked where she was at in selecting a coach. She said I was the only coach she was considering. She had been referred to me by another client. I was flattered, but I asked if she would be open to meeting another coach, if only to compare and contrast. She was, and I introduced her to a coach I deeply respect.

She selected the other coach, who was a better fit because of her specialized knowledge in an area critical to the client. I couldn't have been more pleased. Yes, I lost the engagement, but there's a very happy client out there referring people to me. And the coach sends people my way as well!

Once you've made your decision and communicated it, you will need to contract and map out a plan with the coach. That's the topic of the next chapter.

POWER MOVE

Use the simple tool below and you can't miss on your selection of a coach.

COACH SELECTION TOOL

Area:	Coach 1:			Coach 2:		
Education	H	M	L	H	M	L
Experience	H	M	L	H	M	L
Chemistry questions	H	M	L	H	M	L
1.	H	M	L	H	M	L
2.	H	M	L	H	M	L
3.	H	M	L	H	M	L
4.	H	M	L	H	M	L
5.	H	M	L	H	M	L
6.	H	M	L	H	M	L
7.	H	M	L	H	M	L
8.	H	M	L	H	M	L
9.	H	M	L	H	M	L
10.	H	M	L	H	M	L
Mini-coaching session	H	M	L	H	M	L
Overall Evaluation	H	M	L	H	M	L

Reference Comments:

CHAPTER EIGHT

Nail the Details

A goal without a plan is just a wish.

– Antoine de Saint-Exupery

In a recent chemistry meeting, I asked a prospective client what questions he had for me. The executive looked at me blankly and seemed ready to move on to his next meeting. I surmised he may have already decided on another coach and started to pack up. As I was ready to leave, I pitched my question differently. I said, "Many of my clients want to know more about things like confidentiality... when and how your boss will be involved... what to say to your peers and team... how long the program lasts... how often we meet... fees... do any of those interest you?"

"Yes!" His eyes got big and his eyebrows raised. "All of them!"

Of all the topics that come up in early coaching meetings, confidentiality tops the list. Confidentiality is essential to establishing strong mutual trust between client and coach. Without this foundation, coaching will be less effective or even fail completely.

When I was head of HR, I had to fire a coach for a breach of confidentiality. The conversation was so unpleasant the coach got sick and darted to the restroom. She returned to my office, face white, lips tight, obviously stricken. She denied the breach but there was nothing to be done. All the HR executives on my team believed she had betrayed trust by disclosing information she should have kept private. They would never include her on a slate of coaches for consideration.

Although it seems obvious, confidentiality is full of nuance. I'll come back to that topic in a moment. It's crucial to understand proper and improper disclosure during the contracting phase.

Likewise, it's important at the beginning to address a laundry list of other topics.

Let me walk you through the details.

Outcomes

Stephen Covey said we should "Begin with the end in mind."

You likely know what your organization wants you to accomplish in coaching.

I've encouraged you to do some critical thinking on your own.

Now is the time to shape outcomes with your prospective coach. You'll start this process of goal setting at the chemistry meeting, and you'll continue refining outcomes throughout your first sessions, assessments, and creation of the developmental plan.

Remember: Don't even think of jumping into coaching without clarifying your needs. If you're still searching for the right words to capture what you want, the items below are the most common themes in my coaching practice:

Mike's TOP 11 coaching areas

1. Increase collaboration with peers

2. Exert more influence

3. Remedy problem behaviors (negativity, interrogating, boasting, campaigning, withholding, claiming credit, distributing blame, not taking accountability, etc.)

4. Improve communication

5. Increase strategic acumen

6. Enhance execution

7. Prioritize goals and drive your agenda

8. Enhance executive presence

9. Improve interpersonal skills (listening, empathy, and so on) or emotional intelligence

10. Alleviate triggers that cause fight, flight, freeze, or appease responses

11. Improve leadership effectiveness (a catch-all for a wide range of goals)

As the engagement gets underway, you're looking for alignment on outcomes between yourself, your boss, and your coach, and occasionally, other stakeholders such as HR. The coach facilitates that discussion, but you must own the process.

Deliverables

The coach promises to build the process around specific deliverables. Examples:

- Meet biweekly for in-person (or remote) coaching

- Administer, interpret, and debrief specified assessments

- Conduct stakeholder interviews and present written (or oral) summaries

- Collaborate with client to create a development plan

- Facilitate three-way meetings of client, boss, and coach to align on the development plan

- Keep the coaching program on track

- Maintain confidentiality

You might have other commitments you want the coach to include, but these are core.

Duration

How long will coaching last? The process I outlined in Chapter six takes about six months, assuming meetings every two to three weeks for about an hour. As a reminder, the steps are:

Outcomes	Month 1
Assessments	Months 2-3
Development Plan	Month 3
Coaching to Plan	Months 4-5
Results/Check-in/Sustainability Plan	Month 6

That doesn't leave much time for change, only two or three months after creating the development plan. A six-month schedule must move with pace and momentum, which most executives appreciate.

Some organizations request three-month coaching engagements, most often due to budget constraints or because the client wants to "see how it goes."

I stopped taking three-month engagements a long time ago. The first two steps in the coaching process take at least two months, leaving almost no time for assembling a plan and practicing new behaviors.

Frankly, a client waiting to see how it goes isn't fully committed to coaching. The engagement is destined for disappointment.

However, in less typical circumstances, a shorter engagement might be effective—like when the development area has already been identified and coaching involves making progress in that area. But as I've mentioned before, making assumptions about what a client needs to work on is problematic. The impulse might come from a 360 or observations by the client or boss. These "skills development" engagements can work, but sometimes a misdiagnosis requires us to back up and do more assessment before we can really move forward.

I also don't believe in long or open-ended engagements. As a former executive, I want the process to move. And conclude. With tangible results.

Long engagements can lose pace and urgency. Open-ended engagements often suit an executive and coach who have grown an unusual partnership that goes beyond coaching. However, I would be wary about fostering an unhealthy dependency on the coach. And the invoices keep coming, of course!

Fees

Fees are often handled by HR in a black box. But you should understand the considerable investment the organization makes on your behalf.

Executive coaching fees vary by the level of person being coached, the coach's background, the nature of the engagement, and the location.

The PWC/ICF study mentioned earlier cites an average hourly fee for executive coaching of $340!

Many coaches charge by the hour. I don't. I instead scope the entire engagement and provide a proposal for the process, deliverables, fees, and expenses. I estimate the number of hours I will spend in coaching, interviewing others, reviewing and debriefing assessments, and other preparation. For a typical six-month engagement using the process I've described, I plan on a total of 35-40 hours with a fee starting in the low five figures. I invoice half up front, half at the end.

This is simpler and better for the client and sponsoring party, because they have certainty on the fees. No one watches the meter, and all we care about is doing the job right. From the coach's perspective, this billing process means that when the client wavers about continuing, they're more likely to press on.

My contracts all have an out so the client (or coach!) can opt out, with provisions for reconciling the final fee.

If the coach you're considering charges by the hour, you'll still want them to provide a proposal and estimate fees for each step.

If there's significant additional work not included in the original proposal, we revisit and decide how to move forward.

Occasionally, a coaching engagement is extended. Sometimes there are obvious factors like the discovery of new issues or the arrival of a new manager. Or the client is promoted and wants help navigating the change.

I usually scope extensions as I do regular engagements, providing a proposal and invoicing once or twice. Occasionally, an extension is more indefinite. The client just wants someone to talk to for a few more months. Or to ensure new behaviors take hold. Or to work more broadly on leading the organization through dramatic change or higher-level strategic agenda. For those, I'll charge hourly or monthly.

In addition to fees, there are often expenses associated with coaching, with the cost of assessments the most common. Providers charge coaches for each individual assessment administered, in addition to charging for coaches to be certified in their tool. I pass on the individual assessment charge (generally $100 to $400 for each assessment) directly to the client with no mark up. The time I spend analyzing the assessment and debriefing it with the client is included in my proposed time and fees. Some assessments require several hours to analyze and another hour or two to debrief properly.

If your coach isn't certified in an assessment your organization requires, they need to get certified, usually at the coach's expense, or identify another coach to conduct the assessment, which can result in additional cost to the client.

Contracting

Larger organizations have their own consulting contracts already vetted with their legal departments. These are generic, with a statement of work at the end specifying the coaching deliverables. This, plus a proposal or summary, generally suffices for most individual coaching engagements. For projects involving more than one internal client or more than one coach, I suggest getting legal help.

It's worthwhile putting the terms of the engagement in writing. Some organizations ask me to supply the agreement. My agreement (a sample coaching contract is in the appendix) covers the following:

- Context
- Objectives
- Term
- Deliverables and timeline
- Roles and responsibilities

- Process
- Fees
- Expenses
- Confidentiality
- Early termination/out-clause
- Governing law
- Signatures

Expectations between sessions

Ad-hoc email exchanges, calls, or meetings pop up when concerns can't wait for the next scheduled session. For example, a client just emailed asking to dialog in the next day or two about an internal job opportunity just presented to him.

There's a balance. I don't want to foster dependence, and I know my clients are resourceful and respectful. So they reach out only when the situation demands. Because there's no additional cost for these sessions in my contract, we're focused on addressing the situation rather than a meter ticking upward.

Roles and responsibilities

It helps to pull together all the to-dos and sum up the roles of each participant in the coaching process. If any of these points are an issue for you or others, make sure to raise your concerns prior to the coaching engagement. Consider including any significant alterations in the contract.

Chapter Eight – Nail the Details

Client	Coach	Boss/Sponsor	HR
Selects coach	Outlines and guides process	Identifies opportunity for coaching	Vets coaches
Commits to active participation	Offers appropriate assessments, feedback, and other resources	Actively participates by giving feedback and showing interest in progress	Consults with boss and client on potential coaching engagements
Involves boss and other stakeholders as appropriate	Partners with client to create development plan	Provides input and support on development plan	Oversees vendor relationship and coach effectiveness
Creates development plan	Reports on progress without violating confidentiality	Reinforces observed changes	Participates in engagements as appropriate
Maintains openness to feedback and makes effort to change	Ensures accountability	Models desired behaviors	Administers contracting and payments
Owns the coaching process	Maintains confidentiality		

Confidentiality

Back to the issue that might be top of mind as you enter a coaching engagement. Common sense says that confidentiality is basic to the coach-client relationship, but in an organizational context confidentiality can become complex, especially if your coach doesn't make standards and expectations clear to everyone involved.

The International Coach Federation has a code of ethics governing many aspects of the coach-client relationship. I've included the section on confidentiality in my Sample Coaching Agreement in the appendix.

My contract contains a confidentiality clause where I make clear to the prospective client, boss, HR, and other sponsors how I handle this important concern.

You can safeguard your own interests by asking about confidentiality in the chemistry conversation, as many of my clients do. Find out in practical terms how your conversations, assessments, and other data will be handled. Your organization might claim rights to more information than you expect because they pay the bill and expect a return on their investment.

The simple answer I give clients is that I treat everything we discuss in a coaching session as confidential, and I won't disclose it to anyone. Likewise, any data we collect though assessments or stakeholder interviews is confidential, and I won't share it with anyone.

Confidentiality caveats

There is a crucial exception. If the client freely—without pressure or coercion—allows me to disclose something, I will. Usually with the client present.

You should also be aware that most coaches report to the company if the client is "actively engaged" and "progress is being made." That's it. If that is an issue for you, discuss it with your coach and organization ahead of time.

If there's a violation of law or company policy, I will disclose that point—after first informing the client—but nothing else. (This is quite rare. It's never happened to me or anyone I know.)

One last caveat: Coach confidentiality is NOT protected the way information is protected with your therapist or attorney. In theory it can be subpoenaed, and a coach cannot protect it. However, this is also beyond rare. I've never heard of a situation where this has occurred.

Stakeholder involvement

As you start with your coach, protecting your privacy and creating a safe place with your coach matters. But there's a counterbalance to this issue. You also want to draw into your coaching process the people who matter to your success.

Though the coach assures confidentiality, you are free to disclose anything you want. I do encourage selective disclosure to boss, peers, and direct reports, as I'll discuss further in the chapter on development planning. By *selectively* disclosing the areas you're working on, others can assist you. They're also more likely to notice and applaud your progress if they know you are working on a new behavior.

No oversharing here. No need to review long 360 reports or psychological assessments with others. A quick summary of learnings and actions suffices.

To sum up, my coaching process has several points in which stakeholders can be involved:

- The **boss or board** should be included at the beginning, outlining objectives for the engagement. They're included in the assessment phase, participating in the 360 and stakeholder interviews. Once a development plan is created, it's helpful to review that document to ensure alignment and support, typically in a three-way meeting with the client, boss, and coach. Finally, near the end of the engagement, the boss can be part of the wrap-up, giving feedback on what's gone well and what areas might need continued or additional focus.

- **Peers** can be wrapped into the assessment phase, providing feedback via an online 360 or interviews or both. They can also be reinterviewed toward the end in a mini-360 to check in on progress. Finally, peers can also be an excellent sounding board and source of in-the-moment feedback during the coaching process.

- **Direct reports**, like peers, can be part of the assessments and mini-360s. Since most executives have more interaction with their direct reports than with others, I encourage clients to talk to their direct reports about their learnings and development areas, asking for their support and to be held accountable. In this way, they also become role models for the people on their teams.

In the chapters ahead on process and change, you'll notice that I strongly advocate having key stakeholders involved in the coaching process. You'll need to find your own balance between confidentiality and the need to handle sensitive information with your desire to change—and to have key people support you and notice your progress.

POWER MOVE

The most common question on roles occurs within the coaching session itself. It's a dance question: **Who leads?**

I've found that clients who lead make the most headway. The way to lead is to be prepared to own the process. If you show up for the session without having given thought to it, you'll get less out of the session. When clients look at me to see where we should start, I view that as my failure. I haven't empowered the client nor set appropriate expectations.

Your most powerful way to lead is to use the Coaching Preparation Session Questions introduced in Chapter six.

Coaching Session Preparation Questions

- How am I doing overall?

- Is there anything from the previous coaching session that we need to follow up on?

- What action(s) did I take since our last session? What were my wins/challenges? If I had "homework," how did that go?

- What do I want to get out of today's coaching session?

- What do I want to report?

- What issues do I want to delve deeper into during our coaching session today? What are the challenges, concerns, achievements, or areas of learning to be addressed?

CHAPTER NINE

Get Feedback

I never lose. I either win or I learn.

– Nelson Mandela

Over the past few years, I've coached nearly twenty senior leaders at one of our country's largest retailers. These executives daily do combat in the battle between brick-and-mortar and online retailers, devising strategies to move fast and appeal to experience-hungry customers who want more than beige walls and stacks of jeans. I've focused on helping these executives adapt to the new world, lead change, and preserve a semblance of personal balance.

My primary contact is a vice president for leadership development, whom I'll call Debbie. A couple of years ago, during a regular trip to the company headquarters, Debbie asked to meet.

We greeted each other and caught up. Debbie then pulled out some printed PowerPoint slides titled "Feedback for Mike."

Excuse me?

Debbie had interviewed my clients and came ready to share. Most of it was thoroughly positive, but the last page had suggestions for improvement.

I was barely listening. I was stuck on the title page. "Feedback for Mike"? What the heck? I hadn't requested feedback. I certainly wasn't open to receiving it. I immediately went to an imaginary place where only perfection is allowed, where I feel threatened by anything less.

Fortunately, in the moment I didn't say anything. I thanked Debbie perfunctorily and stuffed my printout into my leather portfolio. I tried to stuff the whole incident into a mental folder as well, so I could carry on with my clients undistracted.

Back at the hotel bar later that evening, behind a large martini, I slipped out the slides and looked them over. The feedback was pretty good, with plenty of positive comments. The improvement areas were dead on, including an issue I hadn't been aware of.

My clients were coaching their coach. And their leader had given me an enormous gift—honest feedback. It could only help me be better. That was her intent.

She had unknowingly given me a second gift as well—the ability to feel how my clients might feel when I give feedback.

You might be fine with constructive criticism. You maybe even seek it out.

That would make you the exception. Most of us live in an illusory world where no news is good news.

The challenge of receiving and giving healthy critique stops many leaders short. Even in organizations that churn out performance reviews like clockwork, in-the-moment feedback often remains scant. And as I mentioned earlier, the higher you go in an organization, the less authentic input you receive. What little you get is sanitized for your protection!

Don't miss this point: The feedback you receive in your coaching engagement may be your one shot at the real deal. So get every bit you can. You can't mitigate, fix, enhance, or strengthen what you don't know.

It's always better to know.

In coaching, you'll gain feedback and self-awareness from several sources:

- Self-assessment
- 360 instruments
- Stakeholder interviews
- Coach observation

Each approach has utility. Let's explore the details.

Self-Assessment Tools

Thousands of self-assessment instruments compete in the coaching space, each promising insight into executives—leadership style, personality, behavior, motivation, preferences, derailers, emotional intelligence, conflict management, and more. Among the abundance of instruments, your coach likely is certified to administer a select few. Each coach has favorites.

While coaches find this stuff fascinating, I know that pushing a list at you of various instruments with their pros and cons would make you flip to the next chapter. It's more important that you understand why a coach would choose a specific instrument AND what your takeaway should be.

Start with these questions:

- How long have you used this instrument?
- When do you use it—in what circumstances?
- Why did you select it for me?
- What do you like about this tool? What are the downsides?

- What will I gain from it?

- Who is the originator or vendor behind this instrument? What is their expertise?

- Can you show me a sample report?

- How long does the tool take to complete?

- When will you debrief me?

- Are there better instruments available?

Most coaches don't use hokum instruments that yield advice on a level with a self-help quiz you get from a magazine at the grocery store checkout. The best tools are well-researched, statistically reliable, and valid. Many are favorites among coaches because they consistently provide accessible, actionable, executive-level data. If you prefer a tool your coach isn't credentialed to administer, ask if another coach can come in and deliver the debrief. That's not an objectionable request. Everyone learns.

While there are no formal categories of assessments, these groupings are helpful:

Assessment types

- **Psychometric:** Insights into your mindset at work, as in how you show up on your best days as well as potential derailers. Best known are Hogan and CPI.

- **Leadership:** Feedback on leadership styles, including communication. Common examples are DISC, Insights, EQi (emotional intelligence), and StrengthsFinder (now CliftonStrengths).

- **Behavioral:** Data on your actions in specific circumstances. For example, the Kilmann Conflict Inventory.

- **Personality**: Reflections of your motivators and core values, and preferred roles, work environments, and organizational cultures. Examples include IDI, MBTI, and Hogan (MVPI).

My clients seem to derive the most benefit from assessments in the first two groups. Psychometric and leadership instruments don't require a lot of time or expense, yet they yield foundational self-understanding. For most engagements, they're a great start. Adding a 360 instrument or interviews—or both—gives you the data you need to do real work.

Other keys in using assessments:

- Expect to complete assessments early in an engagement, but don't be surprised if your coach introduces a tool later, in response to a specific need.

- Your coach will always debrief your results with you. Anything less than a personalized interpretation and discussion of the data is a misuse of the instrument.

- All assessment data should be treated as absolutely confidential unless you, your coach, and your organization reach a different agreement in advance.

I can't count how many times I've had to remind a supervisor that a client's raw assessment data is confidential. Of course, you can choose to self-disclose, but it's more productive to simply share takeaways. My advice? Don't give your report to others, no matter how interested and well-intentioned they might be.

360 Instruments

Self-assessments grant you a deeper knowledge of yourself—like a look in the mirror. What might be even more useful is seeing yourself as others do—like a look in the window.

The hundreds of 360 instruments and stakeholder interview protocols do just that. They pry open the ol' Johari window and let you observe your blind spots.

With tweaks to the details, the instruments all work the same way. You complete an online questionnaire and invite others who know you well to complete it as well. The questions are predominantly quantitative and easy for respondents to complete, like scoring you from 1 to 5 on your ability to learn from mistakes. As others complete the inquiry form, a report generates behind the scenes, consolidating data so individuals can't be identified. You might hear a 360-instrument referred to as "multi-rater" because others besides you provide input.

Reports require a minimum number of respondents to protect anonymity. Some break out data so you can see feedback from your boss and from peers, direct reports, or others. This granularity is particularly useful when groups see you differently.

All 360 instruments have a point of view, eliciting information based on the leadership philosophy of the vendor of the questionnaire. Some instruments are based on competencies the vendor's research has shown to be essential to leadership effectiveness. Some assess classic leadership styles.

So, in addition to the questions above, I'd add two more questions:

- What does this instrument measure?

- What is the underlying philosophy of this instrument?

A 360 usually offers much more data than self-assessments, because it reports not only your own perceptions but the observations of colleagues. You'll see where you align and any gaps between yourself and others, or among groups of respondents.

Initially, the data can be a bit overwhelming, so I usually break the debrief into two coaching meetings. In the first session, we simply go through the data and I provide interpretation. I then offer an easy tool to continue digesting the data between meetings. At the second session, we discuss major takeaways.

Some key questions to ask yourself as you review assessment results:

- What overall strengths and weaknesses are identified, my absolute highs and lows?

- What recurring themes emerge?

- Where do respondents show strong alignment? Where do opinions diverge?

- Where do I agree with the feedback? Where do I disagree?

- What do I make of all this?

Other points to keep in mind:

- **Customize where possible**. Some 360s give you the opportunity to solicit feedback for a question or two of your own.

- **Everyone has high scores and low scores**. Welcome to the human race!

- **The purpose is developmental**. Your organization might conduct annual performance reviews that include 360 feedback. This isn't that. A 360 in the context of a coaching engagement is for development, not evaluation.

- **Ignore outliers**. Ask any group for feedback and you'll get data points that don't line up with the rest. Suppose you get a set of responses woefully lower than everything else. You might assume those marks all came from one person, and you even think you know who it is. Your conclusion might or might not be accurate, but that's unknowable. Frankly, it doesn't matter. It's an outlier. Let it go.

- **Don't lash out.** Occasionally, I fear a client will get 360 feedback and chase down colleagues to give some feedback of their own. If that temptation strikes, ask your coach for healthier ways to process and apply what you discover.

Stakeholder Interviews

The most powerful feedback often comes from one-on-one interviews with a client's boss, peers, and direct reports. I gather information and distill what I hear into themes, protecting confidentiality as with 360s.

Sometimes 360 results don't pinpoint the changes a client needs to make. And the 360's predominantly quantitative data can lack the emotional impact that moves a client to act.

One client, a new R&D director for a well-known consumer product company, had completed and debriefed self-assessments and a 360. From my perspective as his coach, the data should have hit like a sack of bricks to the face. He had serious interpersonal issues.

He just didn't get it.

Until we debriefed the stakeholder interviews.

Feedback normally takes 90 minutes. I budgeted three hours. We needed almost four.

It was the toughest feedback I've ever given. This good person had terrible habits. He was a poor listener, cutting off or talking over others. He spewed constant sarcasm. He undermined. He gave his people incomplete information. He delegated the same task to multiple people. He monopolized credit for results. He seemed to care mostly about himself.

He justified or rationalized some behaviors. He was ignorant of others.

Chapter Nine – Get Feedback

Now he got it.

With eyes red from beginning to end of our initial debrief, he grew uncharacteristically quiet. It took two more agonizing meetings before he stopped resisting his colleagues' feedback. I was as gentle and supportive as I could be without softening my report.

Your stakeholder feedback won't be this difficult. I can 100% guarantee it! But you'll learn things about yourself that you can't get any other way, just as I did when Debbie surprised me with feedback.

The stakeholder interview process starts with selecting participants. Your boss is a must, plus four or five peers and four or five direct reports. I highly recommend that you and your boss go over the list of prospects together to preempt objections later that someone was left out. Including a range of coworkers is essential to good feedback, including a sample of those on the opposite side of key issues. Your boss can weigh in on the mix.

With a final list of participants in hand, you send a brief invitation to each person and inform them your coach will be scheduling a meeting with them. The meeting lasts about 30 minutes, usually by phone.

I'm always surprised at the openness people display. I'm a stranger, a disembodied voice on the phone, but they willingly share information they often haven't communicated to the client, someone they work with closely.

Now you know why coaches exist. Honestly, I'd happily give up coaching if people could learn to consistently communicate feedback.

I ask each participant the same questions. A full list is in the appendix. Here are areas I cover:

- Strengths

- Weaknesses/blind spots

- Managing up/sideways/down
- Influence
- Communication
- Interpersonal skills
- Executive presence
- Handling conflict
- Setting vision and strategy
- Execution
- Reaction under stress or when mistakes are made
- Integrity
- Decision-making

My reports highlight both strengths and development areas, and clients are often just as surprised by how people view their strengths. Discovering a positive blind spot is a gift.

Observation and Shadowing

Occasionally, it helps a client if I observe them in action. This happens most commonly when we work on presentation skills or executive presence, and I can sit off to the side, watch them do their thing, and pay attention to how others react.

Rarely, I've attended a staff meeting to watch the client lead and interact with the team. It's usually unhelpful. I'm sure you can picture everyone snapping into their best behavior.

Thankfully, clients behave in coaching meetings just as they do at their jobs. It's like catching lightning in a bottle. I pause and remark on what I've just observed. This is incredibly powerful because the client can see in real time exactly what others see. We can also analyze what may have triggered that behavior.

In all these scenarios, the coach has one job. Tell the Truth. Not Minnesota Nice Truth, the kind where you must dig around in a pile of fluff to find it, but Truth Undistorted.

Demand this from your coach.

I usually start in one of the following ways:

- Can I give you some feedback you might find useful, but could make you uncomfortable?

- I'd like to give you some observations. I'd suggest you take some time to digest, and not react right away. Are you willing to do that?

- Can we pause? I'd like to react to what just transpired.

Then we dig deeper:

- How do people react to (that tone, those words, that body language) at work?

- What effect do you think your response might have on others?

It might surprise you that many coaches are uncomfortable delivering tough feedback. I am. I'm a nice guy. I want to be liked. It's a weakness. And I don't particularly like intense emotion or conflict. This describes many coaches. We're feelers.

If you suspect that you're not getting all the feedback you need, here's a question to ask your coach:

- Are you telling me everything? Are you holding back anything?

Thinkers can have their issues giving feedback as well. They take the hammer out of the glove and pound away. This variety of coach thinks they're doing you a service by letting you have it, believing you won't hear it otherwise.

You don't have to just take it if it gets brutal. This is personal development, not demolition. Here's what you can tell your coach in these situations:

- I get the feedback. It's difficult for me to hear it. Let me digest it a bit, and we'll come back to it.

Later, after the emotion has subsided, you can give your coach feedback on their delivery:

- I appreciate the direct feedback and will act on it as appropriate. I did think you were pretty tough on me. In the future, can you....

Hang In There

Hearing feedback takes energy. You might get more developmental input during a coaching engagement than you get in many years at work.

The value of feedback is directly related to how you receive it. Many people react with the SARA sequence:

Shock (or Surprise)

Anger

Resistance

Acceptance

The sooner you get to acceptance and embrace the feedback, the more progress you make. Remember, feedback is a rare gift. It crystalizes how others see you. It's up to you to decide what fits and what to do about it. Your best bet is to stay curious. Just get to know this person—*you*—better.

The key is to stay curious. We are all on a road of self-discovery.

With this feedback in hand, you'll work with your coach to determine key areas for development and action planning, the topic of the next chapter.

POWER MOVES

Although feedback is confidential, it's most useful if you can find appropriate places to share it. I encourage clients NOT to share self-assessments, 360 reports, or the results from stakeholder interviews.

For example, I sought feedback as part of my onboarding process when I was hired as CHRO at Ecolab. The company requires all prospective executives to go through a full-day pre-employment selection assessment with an outside firm.

From this assessment I learned a lot about my strengths and development opportunities. After I'd been with the company about a month and we were somewhat acquainted, I discussed what I learned at a staff meeting. I kept it simple: "Based on the feedback, here are the three areas I am working on. I'm telling you what they are, so you can be aware of them. And there are a couple areas where you may be able to help me."

You will be amazed by the impact of this kind of revelation.

- First, demonstrating a continuous improvement mindset is a terrific model for others to follow.

- Second, others welcome the opportunity to support you in your development.

- Third, when you do change, people will be more likely to see it than if you work behind the scenes to get better.

You can try a similar approach with peers. With your boss, I'd encourage going deeper by sharing your Development Plan, which we'll cover next.

CHAPTER TEN

Create Your Development Plan

> *Knowing is not enough. We must apply.*
> *Willing is not enough. We must do.*
>
> – Bruce Lee

Lisa and I had just finished debriefing the last in a series of hard-hitting assessments. Still digesting the feedback she had absorbed over recent sessions, she asked, "What's next? Where do we go from here?"

As you wrap up the assessment phase of your coaching engagement, you'll feel somewhere between ragged and recharged. You're at the crossroads of the coaching process where everything comes together and you transform knowledge into action. "What's next" is creating a development plan that propels you forward.

Some or all of these pulse-checks will feel familiar:

- **You understand more about yourself.** You see your preferences and predilections more clearly. From the murky depths, a blind spot or two has emerged. You sense more viscerally how your behaviors affect others.

- **Most of what you've discovered is worth keeping.** Your strengths have served you well. They got you this far and will power your future success. Your goal is to build on what makes you great without overdoing it.

- **Overused strengths become detrimental.** This is the shadow side of the best of who you are. Chris, for example, is the master of interpersonal finesse. He values the relationship above all else, and most of the time, that works. People fight to work for him, and those fortunate enough to join his team follow him willingly. But his strength becomes a weakness when he hesitates to deliver tough feedback. Or engage in healthy conflict. Or take an unpopular stand. Or make difficult people decisions.

- **Throttling back might be good for everyone.** The drive and relentlessness that propelled you to success might overwhelm your staff if you constantly press urgent demands. Take Chad. With a remarkable capacity for global leadership, he travels the world for his organization at a grueling pace. He perpetually overloads two administrative assistants. He emails his team day and night, expecting instant answers, even on weekends. His exhausted people feel disrespected and mistrusted.

- **Strengths may no longer be strengths.** Behaviors that once earned you accolades can become ineffective as you rise. Kate is known for her command of minutiae, and she excelled at leading her business line by knowing every detail and calling in on every decision. But the multiple line leaders who now work for her want to be trusted to run the business, just as she did when she was in their shoes.

- **You need to grow past your weaknesses.** Michael's abrasive personality and angry outbursts overshadow his absolute analytical brilliance in M&A transactions. His organization has long put up with his behaviors, but people have finally had enough. Even his boss is wondering if he's worth saving.

These points and more are fodder for a development plan. The trick is to revisit your initial goals and assessment takeaways and choose just two or three areas that will make the biggest impact on your success now or in the near future. Consider these your **keystones**. Intervening in these root-cause behaviors, thoughts, beliefs, and habits will create a virtuous cycle that pulls along many other behaviors, thoughts, beliefs, and habits.

As coach, my part of the process is to nudge a client forward without controlling where we go. I filter everything I've learned so far to a few themes. I make time to reflect on what I've observed in our sessions. I come up with clarifying questions specific to the situation. Once the client and I have compared notes, we use our combined leadership intuition to zero in on those two or three high-impact areas.

Here's where good coaches earn their keep. They help clients work raw material into a recognizable shape. They ensure clients see clearly and don't sidestep tough issues.

Let me give you an example of how a client identified a keystone.

Robert, an IT executive, had difficulty managing multiple high-visibility projects, an essential element of his role.

But what was the core issue? We considered several possibilities:

- Setting priorities

- Time management

- Poor organization

- A mish-mash of project management methodologies

- Getting lost in detail

- Taking on too much

- Not saying no

Assessments, interviews, and direct observation helped us realize that above all, Robert was amazingly disorganized. He could get away with that approach on his laptop, where search tools quickly located anything he needed. But it failed in his office space, which looked like a crew of interns had occupied it for a week of all-night work sessions. His intermittent clean-up efforts never lasted.

While adverse behaviors seemed like the root cause, that wasn't the end. Robert enlisted his administrative support person to help him get organized, but he subtly undermined her when she touched anything in his office.

He had a "foot on the brake," that is, an underlying habit, thought, belief, or value causing his problematic behavior. Recognizing and changing this single point could bring positive changes in all the related areas.

What was up? Introspection and dialog revealed that Robert wanted to control everything. Moreover, he pressured himself to have an answer to every question at his fingertips.

Robert believed the best way to stay on top was to save each draft and iteration—of everything. It was no surprise his file cabinets multiplied, desktop stacks toppled, and email attachments filled his hard drive. Yet he acknowledged that he seldom looked back at anything he kept.

Once we understood the real root causes of his disorganization, we generated ideas to shift Robert's thinking. Simultaneously, he worked on behaviors—office organization, priority setting, calendar management. This time, however, the changes were more likely to stick.

We got the darned foot off the brake.

STEP 1: Identify keystones

Creating your development plan is a simple three-step process. The first step matters most of all. You need to define those keystones, your main areas for growth. Some observations:

- **Many coaching clients are preparing for bigger roles and responsibilities.** They write plans to help them move higher, with keystones such as setting strategy, leading change, acting courageously, and driving an agenda.

- **Other clients want to sharpen performance in their current role.** Their plans focus on areas like enhancing interpersonal skills, executive presence, and communication skills.

- **Some executives need to remedy a risk factor.** The company engages a coach to address a potential derailer with a leader who is otherwise effective.

I call this last group "high beta" executives. Lots of upside with huge potential downside. For these leaders, the development plan aims to significantly reduce or even eliminate problem behaviors.

Those problem behaviors often fall at opposite ends of a spectrum. At one extreme, you might see abrasiveness, outbursts, or intense scrutiny and questioning that borders on interrogation. At the other extreme, there might be timidity, reluctance to take a stand, or disappearing into the conference room woodwork.

One further note. Some coaches and clients only want to build on strengths. Others only want to work on weaknesses. I think either extreme is a mistake. Your development plan should reflect both, further enhancing strengths while curtailing weaknesses.

SOAR analysis

The areas you want to work on might be obvious. If you want to approach this task with more rigor, you can perform a **SOAR** analysis (Strengths, Opportunities, Aspirations, Results). This simple self-assessment considers the data and feedback you've received, along with introspection about where you want to go.

SOAR ANALYSIS

STRENGTHS	OPPORTUNITIES/WEAKNESSES
• In what areas do you shine? • What awards and recognition have you received? • What do you do better than most of your peers? • What do assessments and feedback identify as strengths? • What unique experiences do you bring to your role?	• What new skills do you need in your toolkit? • What experiences do you want? • Where does your current role compel you to develop? • What shortcomings were identified from feedback or assessments? • What additional certifications or training does your current or next role require?
ASPIRATIONS	RESULTS
• What do you want to do in the future? • What attributes, knowledge, and skills would you like to develop? • To expand your leadership reach, where do you need to grow? • To become an expert and narrow your focus to what you truly love, what needs to happen?	• What does success look like? • How will you measure development results? • What specific accountabilities are you expected to meet? • What metrics do you need to hit for a promotion, recognition, or additional compensation? • What outcomes matter to you that might not matter to anyone else?

Your SOAR Analysis can sum up the reams of data you've received, capturing the highlights on a single page. It should enable you to identify your two to three keystones.

Focus!

Why just two to three keystones? Because one isn't enough and four is too many.

I'm serious. Change is hard. Focus is essential. If you want to err, do it on the side of concentrated effort toward a single goal. Applying yourself in one area rather than four guarantees you'll see more progress sooner. Success begets success, and you can always circle back and repeat the process.

Once you've identified keystones, test them with your boss. This is the right moment for a three-way meeting with you, boss, and coach, reviewing development areas and action steps in a draft plan.

You'll get a good reality check. Plus buy-in from the most important person in your work. And your boss needs a heads up to see and support change.

STEP 2: Identify action steps

You could dive in and do any of thousands of potential action steps. The vast assortment may leave you stymied.

Start by thinking beyond the usual growth activities.

Books are supplements, quick paths to knowledge. Trainings and workshops can be a safe place to acquire and practice new skills. But once you shut the book or head back to work, the learning rarely sticks.

Most research says that 70% of leadership development occurs on the job. Easy to say, but how can you build a development plan with on-the-job activities?

Start with what you already know. You're best positioned to identify growth opportunities at work. If you want to improve your presentation skills, for example, where can you do that?

Second, tap your coach for ideas and resources. Reference books such as the *Successful Executive Handbook* contain a wealth of help.

Third, ask your boss about upcoming opportunities. This inquiry can happen before or during the three-way meeting.

In the appendix are ideas for experiences in core development areas:

JOB	Projects
	Temporary jobs
	Fill-ins for someone else
	Presentations
	Start-up
	Turnaround
	Task force
	Customer engagement
	Product launches
	Analyses
	Strategy development
PEOPLE	Mentors
	Role models
	Teachers
	Board of advisers
	Shadowing
LEARNING	Training
	Workshops
	Seminars
	Programs
	Reading

OUTSIDE	Volunteer
	Community
	Boards
	Toastmasters
	Networking

Practicing Behaviors

Some development activities are obvious. If you want to be more strategic, then join a task force charged with generating and executing a plan. Combine that with readings or a workshop on strategy. And shadow someone in your organization known for a strategic mindset.

Other opportunities need to be embedded throughout your existing work. Better listening skills or exhibiting greater sensitivity, for example, grow best through moment-by-moment practice, often with the people who know you best. As Gandhi supposedly said, "Be the change you wish to see in the world." Combine deliberate daily practice with reading, workshops, frequent feedback, and reflection.

The keys to designing effective behavioral change actions are:

- You're willing to do them.

- You can build them into a routine.

- They'll cause the desired effect.

That's so straightforward it sounds beyond basic. But in practice, this is where we fail. We don't do. We try once, then forget. Or we try and fail. Sound familiar?

I use a checklist for actions to raise the probability of success:

- ☑ I can put them on my to-do list.

- ☑ I can enlist an accountability partner to regularly check my progress.

- ☑ I have a system to remind myself, even something as simple as sticky notes.

- ☑ I have a buddy to practice with me or support me.

- ☑ I reflect for a few minutes each day on what I tried, how it went, and what I want to do tomorrow.

Pausing to size up what you're trying to accomplish can help. Do you remember trying to pick up a new language? Or learning to ski or golf or play a musical instrument? Were you a master of the art the first time?

It takes practice to gain competence. The 10,000-hour rule made the Beatles the Beatles. They played gig after gig in Germany before landing in America. Bill Gates had unlimited access to a school computer and spent nights riffing code before he came up with MS-DOS. It's the same for anyone at the top of what they do.

The practice you do toward your development is like conducting little experiments. Try new behaviors long enough to see if they achieve the desired outcome. If they do, GREAT! If not, move on. Plan on a process of trial and error. Learn what works for you. Leadership is *practice*. Consider it *play*.

The good news is that you won't need 10,000 hours to get competent, unless you're launching a rocket or doing brain surgery. But mastery requires time plus tolerance for making mistakes. Stay light and go easy on yourself.

STEP 3: Define success metrics

Once you've identified keystones and selected activities that allow you to practice, there's one more thing to do. Define success. What will it look like? If you raise your game, what will you see? What will others notice? And what value will you create for yourself and your organization?

I use a simple one-page development plan to capture these three steps. It's my format of choice because it puts everything on one page for easy reference. You can tuck it in a folder and glance at it throughout your day. If you prefer a more detailed step-by-step format, check the appendix.

Development plan for _____

Development goals	Specific development actions	Success metrics/timing	Results

You'll see one final column on this form, Results. Fill it in as you go.

Sharing Your Plan

I strongly encourage you to share portions of your plan. Many people gave feedback via an online 360 or interviews. Many more already know you're working with a coach. At minimum, thank them for participating. Beyond that, I also recommend sharing a few high-level themes—the keystones you're working on. You don't need to share your whole plan. Doing this will:

- Prime them to see change

- Encourage them to hold you accountable

- Invite them to be part of your crew to help you over the rough spots

Unfortunately, people often don't notice change in others. We just aren't that observant. I shaved my beard three days ago, but my wife has yet to notice!

I've heard it said that you need to change 100% for people to see a 10% change. Don't get hung up on the percentages. Just know that the precept seems to hold. You need to change A LOT for people to see A LITTLE. By prepping people to see change, they're more likely to notice when it happens.

POWER MOVES

Use this development plan checklist so your Plan has POWER. You will change, and others will see it!

Development Goals

- [ ] Focused on two or three keystone areas needed for current or future jobs
- [ ] Shared with manager and incorporated input
- [ ] Focused on both strengths and development gaps
- [ ] A little out of comfort zone

Action Steps

- [ ] Clear action plan
- [ ] On to-do list
- [ ] Mostly on-the-job experiences
- [ ] Supplemented by learning in books, training, etc.

Success Measures

- [ ] Shared with others to get support
- [ ] Realistic and measurable
- [ ] Milestones to stay on track

CHAPTER ELEVEN

Make Change Stick

*Yesterday I was clever,
so I wanted to change the world.
Today I am wise,
so I am changing myself.*

– Rumi

Despite Jim's capable leadership of operations at a large health system, his behavioral issues had resulted in several HR investigations. His aggressive and inappropriate comments in a highly regulated, unionized environment threatened to crash an otherwise strong contributor.

The HR executive coordinating Jim's coach selection relayed that the situation was dire, and she wondered if I thought he could amend his behaviors. In my chemistry meeting with Jim, he too asked whether I believed he could change. Then, half a breath later, he told me he didn't want to! When I asked him to clarify, he said he would never budge on who he was at his core.

I'll tell you what I say to anyone struggling with change: You don't have to abandon the real you. Rather, you need to try new behaviors and broaden your range of options, so that in any situation, you can consciously choose the most effective behavior. In current lingo, you'll be more *agile*.

Change is hard. Period. Whether you're attempting to stop problem behaviors or start and sustain positive new ones, you're constrained by your potent values and beliefs on one hand and by your equally formidable habits on the other.

Inertia is a cruel reality.

Meyer's Change Triangle

To be human means to have difficulty admitting our need for change. And even when we desperately want to think, feel, or act differently, we don't know how.

Paradoxically, we're all changing, every day. We're getting older, and as Rumi hopes, wiser. The real question isn't "Can I change?" but "Can I change my behavior in a positive, intentional way AND sustain that change over time?"

The worth of a coach and the success of an engagement are measured primarily by the positive, enduring changes visible in the client. Coaches know change is damned hard, even for highly motivated and capable executives. It's especially challenging when they need to adjust part of what made them successful.

I believe change happens in the context of three drivers of behavior: **head** (thoughts and beliefs), **heart** (feelings and intuition), and **hands** (habits and behaviors).

For lasting change, you need to address each point of the triangle as well as the interactions between each point. Obviously, the content of your thoughts affects what you do or how you feel. Conversely, however, what you do affects also how you feel and what you think. And what you feel affects your thoughts and behaviors.

MEYER'S CHANGE TRIANGLE

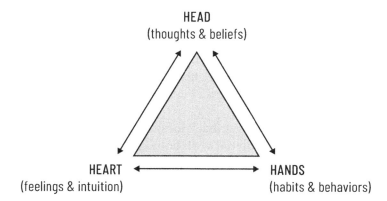

Changing one point can change the other two. For example, if you change a behavior, your thoughts and feelings may follow over time. Likewise for the other two points.

However, in a bizzarro opposite world, if you try to change one point without changing the other two, you can meet internal resistance. If you modify a behavior while believing you were doing it right all along, in no time you'll revert to the original behavior.

What we need is a coordinated approach to sustained change, simultaneously working on the head, the heart, and the hands. We need a plan. We need tools. And we need help.

THOUGHTS: Master your inner dialog

One of the most talented executives I ever coached was in the CEO succession pool of a large medical device firm. Blake's towering strengths had elevated him to a lofty level. He was flat-out smart. Extraordinarily strategic. Engaging in the extreme. He built relationships at all levels of the organization, all over the world. When he set a course, people naturally followed, buying into his urgency and drive for results.

Blake had the whole package.

And then some.

Unfortunately, he employed some of his strengths to excess. Bragging that he slept only four hours a night, Blake sent a nonstop barrage of requests that drove a team of 14 direct reports to distraction.

That was just one point of feedback for Blake summarizing over two dozen interviews I conducted with colleagues and team members past and present.

As we worked together, I discovered Blake's behavior was intransigent, driven by thoughts he wasn't fully acquainted with. In his way of thinking, his behavior had vaulted him to the top of a premier organization. By changing, he would cease to perform at his current level, and he would have to give up his ambitions. Blake feared becoming...mediocre.

Our first job was to uncover those thoughts. Once brought into the light of day, they could be challenged and replaced. We concurrently changed some of his more egregious behaviors, like Sunday emails. Over time, he was able to soften this pacesetting style somewhat.

Old thoughts often hold back change. But here's what the process looks like when I help clients challenge and replace unhelpful ways of seeing the world:

- **I raise awareness when people don't want to change.** I make the point that they don't have to abandon the essence of who they are. Chances are good that they're quite fond of that person! They simply need to broaden their range of options to use as they see fit.

- **I invite people to explore their beliefs to see if they still work.** Many times, clients aren't aware of their thoughts and beliefs, and if they are, they haven't examined whether those beliefs still serve them. To quote the all-time favorite question of a friend and long-time coach, "How's that workin' for ya?" (I think he learned that from Dr. Phil.)

- **I help people replace existing beliefs with new ones.** For example, if a client fears that "If I change, I'll lose what makes me effective," we might replace it with "If I have more options, I can choose what will make me most effective."

Neuroscience says the brain produces 70,000 thoughts every day...3,000 per hour...about 50 a minute...one every second or so.

Who knew?

The brain is a thought machine. That's what it does for a living, and it's a pretty good producer. Unfortunately, when production is high, there's not much quality control. The brain loves volume.

Studies say that of our 70,000 thoughts, three-quarters are negative, a sad mental habit the recovery movement has long labeled "Stinkin' Thinkin'."

We heap scorn on ourselves, letting emotion cloud our thoughts. We catastrophize, complaining there's no end to whatever we endure. We generalize, making a specific incident universal. We personalize, making a situation all about us.

These thoughts are particularly insidious in preventing change. I'm calling them out so you can spot them and put them in their place:

Mike's Stinkin' Thinkin' List

I can't do this.
I'll look foolish (or stupid or incompetent) if I try.
People will realize I'm an idiot.
I'm going to screw this up.
As long as I messed up, I might as well give up.
I never do this right.

Aren't I the greatest?
I'm so much better than...
I'm such a loser.
I always....
I never....
If I'm not perfect, I'm a failure.
I should...
I shouldn't...
I don't belong here.
I'm a fraud.
He hates me.
She's jealous of me.
I know beyond any doubt that...
He did that because...

(Add your own thoughts...)

You know you're engaging in Stinkin' Thinkin' when you reject data that refutes you. When your inner self erupts on others in name-calling, labeling, and blaming. When your lack of confidence erodes decision-making and triggers all manner of unproductive behaviors.

Stinkin' Thinkin' runs in the background on a continuous loop, ruminations that create cognitive ruts.

It. Never. Shuts. Up.

Stopping Stinkin' Thinkin'

The first step to disempowering Stinkin' Thinkin' is to recognize it. Because these automatic thoughts flit in and out of your conscious mind, your first task is awareness, exposing and admitting the thinking. Enter the power of assessments, feedback, dialoging with a coach, and experimenting with new thoughts and behaviors—all of which help you notice unhelpful thoughts.

Once you recognize a thought, you diminish its impact by reducing, overriding, or replacing it. Some techniques:

Dispute the thoughts. Learn to argue with yourself. This technique, first developed by psychologist Alfred Ellis in the 1950s, still works today. Coaches love it. Some specific techniques to dispute your thinking:

Ask yourself for evidence. When your brain overreacts, exaggerates, or replays old tapes, determine the facts. The evidence and data almost always contradict the negative thought and prove it factually incorrect.

Key question: What's the evidence for this belief?

Seek alternative explanations. Instead of browbeating yourself or assuming the worst, look for other explanations. Ask yourself what you would tell a friend in a similar situation. Ask what a friend would tell you.

Key question: Is there a less destructive way to look at this?

Determine implications. Even if the thought is partly correct, your fears may be overblown. De-catastrophize. Gain perspective. Ponder the real implications. Ask yourself how important the issue at hand will be in a week, month, or year.

Key question: So what? What's the worst case?

Ask if the thought is useful. If it's destructive, discard it. Even if it contains a kernel of truth. Substitute a more useful belief that encourages positive action. Then get on with your day.

Key question: What would be a more helpful belief?

Distance yourself from your explanation. If a drunk or a jealous rival yelled these things at you, would you believe them? Of course not. You would chalk them up as crazy talk. It's far easier to distance ourselves from the unfounded accusations of others than from ourselves. Because they come from inside, we inherently trust them.

Be curious about your thoughts, as if they belong to someone else. Stand back. Momentarily suspend belief. Check for accuracy.

Affirmations. Daily affirmations, gratitude journals, and positive thinking build a reservoir to draw on. Keep files of emails or cards others send you. Hang posters on your wall or tuck notes in your briefcase. Do whatever works to reinforce the positive and enhance your resilience.

Distract yourself. Here's a quick defense in the heat of the moment when you don't have time for other methods. Simply tell yourself to stop the thinking. You can write down the thought to address later, which causes your brain to stand down and stop repeating. Or make an appointment with yourself to analyze the thought. Then distract yourself with other activities or immerse yourself in whatever is unique or unusual about the person or situation you're dealing with. In other words, be present.

Dismiss it. Visualize the thought as a cloud passing over. Remind yourself, "What a silly thought!" Or "There my brain goes again!"

FEELINGS: Stop reacting

I'm ashamed to admit that I once got so heated with a customer service agent at the cable company—over a trifle—that I had to beg him not to disconnect my service. Ugghhh.

Triggers cause a strong emotional reaction based not only in our constant stream of thoughts but also more subtle emotions. When we're flush with feelings that are difficult to manage, gaining awareness of what's going on inside helps us hit pause and make deliberate choices.

Thought and emotion often play on each other. We feel something, then generate thoughts to interpret, rationalize, or justify the feeling. Or a thought pushes us into emotional reaction. Example:

- I get angry because someone doesn't do what I want, and I then justify my anger by thinking that person is incompetent.

- I think someone is incompetent, and I therefore react angrily when they don't deliver something as promised.

Life continually confronts you with situations, circumstances, and events that can cause you to react. When you're triggered, how would an onlooker describe your response? Sharp, volatile, even explosive? Or calm, measured, and thoughtful?

Are you managing your emotions, or are your emotions managing you?

Many of my clients get triggered and react emotionally without considering the impact on others. They're playing the short game. Stimulus meets response. Like Pavlov's salivating dogs.

We can all be better than that. We must be.

Feelings, however, can be the most difficult of the three areas to address. Many people complain they can't change their feelings, because "feelings just happen." That's partly true. Feelings are indeed a reaction to stimuli, either external (stuff happens) or internal (thoughts or subconscious rumblings). While we can't change what happens, we can choose our response.

By responding with full self-awareness instead of a knee-jerk, you give yourself choices.

Viktor Frankl, the concentration camp survivor, psychologist, humanitarian, and author of *Man's Search for Meaning*, believed that,

"Between stimulus and response, there is a space. In that space is our power to choose our response. In our response lies our growth and our freedom."

Unfortunately, a reflex can be disastrous. A careless word, gesture, or facial expression can alienate the best of friends and turn people on the fence into enemies. Your future can be determined by the emotions of the moment.

You can learn to identify, expand, and use the space Frankl spoke of. I teach my clients a simple four-step STOP process to increase their capacity to manage emotional reactions.

STOP Process

STOP what you're doing.

TAKE three deep breaths. Use 4/7/8 breathing, a mix proven to calm the nervous system. Inhale to a count of four, hold for a count of seven, and exhale for a count of eight. Repeat three times.

OBSERVE your feelings. Put a name on your emotion. While you're paying attention, what physical sensations are you experiencing? What values, beliefs, or thoughts are interjecting? Of all the things swirling inside, what's helping you—or causing harm?

PROCEED with your best response. Ask yourself, "What are my options?" Say it aloud if you need a reminder—you ALWAYS have options. Then choose a reaction that aligns with your longer-term goals and highest values. Your mantra might be "Play the Long Game"!

Amazingly, in many situations, you can STOP in a split second. That's all it takes to respond with your best self. In more difficult or intense situations, it might take more time.

If you have children, especially teen children, you've been triggered. On purpose. It's hormonal. It's a game. It's fun! Next time your teen triggers you, try the STOP process and watch what happens. I guarantee two things: a bewildered teen and, over time, an improved relationship.

HABITS: Act now

Author Steven Pressfield says, "We can never free ourselves from habits, but we can replace bad habits with good ones." He knew this as well as anyone. He spent years developing a writing habit before he became successful.

You need habits to function. Without them, you would be overwhelmed by the million daily actions and decisions required to survive. Imagine driving without ingrained routines. Or having to think about brushing your teeth. If you really want to mess with yourself, stop and ponder each step as you walk. Habit makes many bits of life almost effortless, and the fact that they run silently is what makes them effective. Because they run in the background, however, we might overlook their power.

Nobel Prize winner Daniel Kahneman describes two primary awareness systems of the human body:

- **System 1: Fast and automatic.** This habit-based system governs 80% of our daily activities. We need this system to be fast and efficient. Multiply 5 X 5, and your fast system jumps into action.

- **System 2: Slow and deliberate.** This deep-thinking system can override System 1, but the effort requires a lot of energy to do that. Multiply 253 by 971, and unless you're a human calculator, your slow system comes online.

We tend not to use the slow system unless we really need it. But with training, we can bring the slow system into operation. And we need System 2 to change the patterns of System 1.

At first, change requires planning and considerable effort to swap an ineffective or even destructive habit with a more effective one.

The goal is to replace that old habit with a new and improved variation because the effort needed to repeatedly tap System 2 is too burdensome. You can't always depend on System 2, particularly when you're tired, stressed, upset, or otherwise depleted. When your reserves are down, it's highly difficult to muster the energy to escape old habits. Can you see why and when you're most vulnerable?

Charles Duhigg's *The Power of Habit* explains the human habit loop with the following diagram:

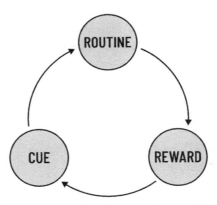

- Habits start with a **cue**—a trigger. The alarm rings. The coffee pot boils. Your smartphone dings.

- The cue precipitates a **routine**—a habit. You silence the alarm and crawl to the shower. You pour the coffee. You check your phone for messages.

- The behavior is reinforced by **reward**—an internal sense of well-being, perhaps accompanied by an external smile. Your tiredness washes down the drain. You savor each sip. You hit send on a witty email response.

Over time, habits become self-reinforcing and very resistant to change. When your whole system of values, beliefs, and good feelings support a habit, you end up with a strong behavioral system. Without that support, well, that's why changing a habit without examining the rest of the system often ends in failure.

In practical terms, your first steps to changing an established behavior are to

- become aware of your habit (what automatic response is kicking in?)
- recognize the cue that causes the habit to kick in (what causes the predictable response?)
- identify the reward you get from the habit (what result do I get from this habit?)

There's a catch. Theorists say it's almost impossible to change the cue or the reward in the habit loop. Most suggest the only way to interrupt the habit loop is to swap the routine while leaving the cue and reward intact.

Given that reality, to overcome an existing behavior we need to substitute a competing response:

The habit I want to change: _____

When this happens (cue): _____

Instead of doing this (old response): _____

I will do this (new response): _____

It's possible to manage the cues—sometimes, with occasional success.

For example, I've shut off all the alerts on my smart phone, so when someone emails or texts, I don't get an aural cue. Theoretically, that should put me in charge of when I check my phone. I say theoretically, because the darn thing is so powerful, I still check it compulsively.

To really get at this habit, I had to further control the cue. I tried shutting off my phone or putting it in airplane mode, so I give people my complete attention. That indeed resulted in fewer cues to check messages, although I still catch myself reaching into my pocket for my phone. It's like checking your wrist for the time when you're not wearing a watch. Hard habits to break.

Further complicating the mix, some deeply rooted habits go way back. Something long ago kickstarted a habit. Or parents passed down set ways of doing things that are no longer productive.

Many of my clients wonder about the origins of their quirks and patterns. As a coach I focus on the here and forward. How is a habit serving you now? Do you want to change? How much? What triggers your routine? How do you benefit? What could you substitute?

Putting It All Together

Maybe you're wondering what happened with Jim, whose story started this chapter. The good news? He's still employed. The reality? He continues to struggle with ingrained habits. Change hasn't happened overnight. But he has two tools he didn't have before we met.

First, he has greater self-awareness. He now knows *before* he says or does something that might get him into trouble. He's trained himself to sense the cues. He feels his body react. And his thought patterns no longer control him.

Second, he has a range of methods to avoid the problem. He can choose different actions. He breathes. He walks the long route to a meeting.

He pauses before he speaks and chooses more careful words. And he accepts correction when he doesn't get it right.

Jim has become a better listener. He's slower to interrupt, and he's completely stopped the wisecracks that put people off.

When Jim feels spent, he's particularly vulnerable to backsliding. That's true for all of us. When we're depleted—tired, upset, distracted, overloaded, stressed, or worse—we don't have the reserves and resilience we wish we had. Those situations call for taking special care with what we say, do, and decide.

You can learn to scan yourself and take inventory. When your battery runs low, adjust your expectations of yourself and others. And figure that change will happen in a sawtooth pattern. You'll have up days and down days. But your overall trend is up and to the right.

POWER MOVES

Here are a few accountability-focused moves that will help you to make and sustain change:

- **Tell others what you're trying to change.** Ask them for feedback both in the moment and in regularly scheduled meetings.

- **Find a buddy or a coach to hold you accountable.** Marshall Goldsmith talks about having someone call you every night to ask you to grade yourself on your development goals.

- **Attach a new, desired habit to an old one.** Do you get a coffee every day at 2pm for an afternoon boost? Why not attach a new habit to that and walk by people's desks to engage them in conversation? A client used that simple technique to overcome natural introversion and informally engage with team members more frequently.

- **Count your habits.** Sometimes, we're simply not aware of our habits. At Toastmasters, an organization dedicated to improving presentation skills, attendees count the "UMs" in a presenter's speech. The presenter becomes more self-aware and gradually learns to stop the distracting habit.

- **Breathing.** My clients love the 4/7/8 breathing discussed above. Inhale for a count of four, hold for seven, exhale for eight. This habit helps derail emotions and reactions that don't serve you well.

CHAPTER TWELVE

Stay on Track

> *The great thing in the world is not where we stand, but in what direction we are moving.*
>
> – William James

At the start of a coaching engagement, only one question really matters:

What will make this coaching engagement a success?

I help the client crystallize the answer to that question right from the start. I raise it in the chemistry meeting. I ask it again on an intake form my clients complete before coaching commences. We discuss the question thoroughly at our first meeting, and we repeatedly circle back to it to ensure we're on track. I also ask the boss/sponsor the same question. All of us need to be aligned on what success looks like.

As you move deeper into your coaching engagement, however, another question rises to the top:

Am I maximizing this opportunity?

You know better than anyone whether you're doing all you can to grow and reach your goals. But your coach also has a keen perspective on your dedication to the process. Organizational sponsors and other stakeholders are also measuring you against their expectations. Your best answer to this "maximization question" considers all three points of view:

CHECKPOINT ONE: Your gut

Be honest with yourself. How is coaching going? What are you getting out of the experience? What more do you want? What will it take for you to squeeze every last bit of value out of it?

CHECKPOINT TWO: Your coach

Your coach has been at this place more times than you know, with enough clients to discern whether you're making progress or falling behind. Many clients reach a tipping point where they realize the insights of a good coach are more than opinion. They're evidence-based and deserve serious consideration. What your coach knows derives from listening to others—in 360s, shadowing, or three-way meetings that bring in your boss. That knowledge is also grounded in observing YOU—session after session.

If you aren't on pace, your coach knows. You should be getting competent, honest, targeted feedback for your consideration and action; now is the time to make sure you're letting it all in.

CHECKPOINT THREE: Your boss

You might feel like you're making tremendous progress, while stakeholders think you're just inching forward. Nowhere near the finish line.

Few coaching goals are *quantifiable*, but behavioral changes are *observable*. It's reasonable to assume that when you experience the growth that executive coaching brings about, visible results will follow. So when others measure your progress, do they like what they see?

Here's what is going on: Measuring change is relative. In other words, incremental or gradual change tends not to be noticed by others.

You can combat that by over-indexing, at least for a while. Turn up the volume on your changes until you settle into a new, better normal.

For example, I once was told I needed to improve my leadership game in the area of communication. My boss said I needed to AMP IT UP. When I did as he asked, I felt like I was screaming. Others? They thought my volume knob was set around five. The only place my forcefulness was a 10 was inside my own head.

I encourage people to over-correct. Find your 11. Remember that you need to change a lot for others to notice. You can pull back later.

Move Fast, Move Far

In the end, you're accountable to yourself, your coach, and your stakeholders for results. So as you look toward the finish line of your coaching engagement, are you struggling—or succeeding?

I know why clients ultimately succeed—and why they don't.

The following factors determine how fast and far you'll go in reaching your goals. When you've got these things going for you, you can expect success:

- **Accountability:** You take responsibility for change and results. You make the most of the accountability built into the process using assessments, check-ins, and follow-up.

- **Self-awareness:** You throw open the Johari window and gain insight into yourself as well as how others see you. You're responsive to all the tools and techniques your coach employs to help you increase self-awareness.

- **Motivation:** You're motivated to change. You deeply want to improve, and you devote time and energy to the process.

- **Specific goals:** Your coaching goals are SMART—Specific, Measurable, Achievable, Relevant, and Time-based.

- **Involvement:** You bring others into what you're learning. You communicate select development areas, seeking feedback and asking for support.

- **Openness:** You're receptive to input. You're game to try new behaviors even if they feel awkward at the start.

Spinning in Place

When coaching isn't successful, it usually isn't *un*successful. That isn't coaching double-speak. Coaching rarely tanks completely, though I will discuss the nature of true failure below. What happens more often is that you get stuck, spinning in place with little or no forward motion.

These indicators suggest your coaching experience will be gauged as ineffective:

- **Obligation:** You entered coaching just to check the box. You're participating against your will, and you aren't really interested in changing.

- **Slacking:** You're not reflecting or practicing between meetings, so your only session preparation happens five minutes before your coach shows up. You don't do the homework.

- **Distraction:** You frequently reschedule and/or cancel. Your on-again, off-again attention to your program leads to lost momentum, cadence, and rhythm.

- **Downgrading:** Being coached drops to the bottom of your priority list. Maybe it falls off completely.

- **Disconnecting:** You shut out the stakeholders you need to be successful.

Most of the factors that cause coaching to succeed or spin are within your control, so that you alone determine how your engagement pans out. As with anything, you get out what you put in.

Getting Back on Track

As you might have concluded from the last chapter, I'm not a fan of the "Just Do It" philosophy of human growth. There's more to it than that. If you're falling short of what you want out of your coaching engagement, go back and reread that chapter. Then try these ideas to help you reenergize:

Challenge any excuses. Do some soul searching. Look back at the Coaching Readiness Curve in Chapter five. Score yourself now, from "I'm actively resisting" to "I'm all-in." Then work through these questions, which are especially relevant when you grow frustrated with yourself, or with the expectations of others, or with doing the hard work of being coached:

- How am I owning my development and this coaching process?

- What progress have I noticed in my thoughts and attitudes?

- How have my external behaviors changed for the better?

- What progress do others see?

- Where am I struggling?
- What external obstacles do I need to remove?
- Are there any warning signals I need to address?
- What can I do to maximize this opportunity?

Revisit your goals. Now that you understand the process and possibilities of executive coaching, you're in a better place to remember and refine your goals. What outcomes would motivate you to move forward?

Some possibilities:

- I want to make a bigger impact.
- I want to be promoted.
- I want to make better decisions.
- I want to be more strategic.
- I want to improve my leadership.
- I want to have a stronger executive presence, or better communication skills, or more empathy, or better interpersonal skills, or (fill in the blank here).
- I want to get rid of bad habits.
- I want to be more courageous.
- I want to develop my people and delegate more to them.
- I want to be more resilient.
- I want better work/life balance.

- I need to be more organized and prioritize better.

- I need help leading the organization through significant change.

- I need help dealing with a difficult situation or a tough boss.

Remember the upside of success. Sure, you can mope around in the unpleasant consequences of mediocre results or outright failure in your coaching engagement. But feeling bad about yourself or the situation rarely motivates enduring change. Instead, list the benefits that will accrue to you if you reach your goals.

Get help. By definition, coaching is a collaborative effort. Don't go it alone. Your coach is your prime resource for your development. But what else do you need? Who can deliver that assistance?

Coaching Misses

Even the most invested client can lose out if others don't play their parts. Among the most common misses is a boss who doesn't get involved, who injects negativity, or who exits the job or company mid-engagement.

An unsupportive boss usually isn't enough, however, to halt your forward progress. When an engagement truly goes south, it's more often because of something the coach does or fails to do. If that happens, it's up to you to call out your coach. Some watch-outs:

- **The coach breaches confidentiality:** When a boss demands details on client, coaches generally keep it simple, with statements like "we're on track" or "we're meeting regularly." That begs more questions. "Does Joe know how his people view him?" "Does Bonnie understand the importance of change?" "Where is Silvia struggling? What can I do to help?" Probing questions can coax a coach to share private information, even inadvertently.

- **The coach breaks trust:** Sharing confidential information often destroys trust beyond repair. More insidious damage occurs when a coach seems to act counter to the client's best interests. Coaches who show off their knowledge, don't pay attention, or believe they know best send the message the client doesn't come first.

- **The coach creates dependency:** A client with an unhealthy reliance becomes reluctant to make decisions without consulting the coach. Or an engagement goes on for *years*, because the coach won't set the client free.

- **The coach has conflicts of interest:** Conflicts take many forms. Does the coach push to extend a gig that's a cash cow? Does the coach have other financial interests in the sponsoring organization? Does the coach receive commissions for using certain materials or assessments? Does the coach have relationships that interfere with the current engagement?

- **The coach is a company stooge:** Picture a boss reluctant to challenge the client or address performance issues. What to do? Get a coach to deliver difficult feedback or other bad news.

- **The coach overloads on advice:** A coach with more answers than questions hinders clients from gaining problem-solving skills. This is an easy trap for coaches! When a client says, "I need your advice," I usually reply, "I try to stay out of the advice business, but let's talk about the challenge you're facing."

If you see any of these issues in your coaching relationship, address it with the coach. In some situations, an adjustment will resolve the issue. If the coach encourages dependency, for example, the engagement might be rescued by setting a definite end date.

There are other instances that demand an immediate end of the coaching relationship. These also call for your HR department to get involved.

- **The coach is abusive:** The coach dominates the relationship, using sarcasm or other verbal abuse to gain control. Or they use power, authority, and manipulation to force the client to do what the coach feels is the right thing. Or the coach is just plain interpersonally toxic. In a more velvet-glove form of abuse, a coach gets a senior executive's ear and wields inappropriate power, like suggesting personnel changes or commandeering business strategy.

- **The coach violates professional boundaries:** A coach who tries to engage in an inappropriate relationship with a client—we've already covered that as a violation of the ICF code of ethics. Run away!

In these extreme situations, extract yourself. Be done without hesitation. End of story.

Break the Tape

Your coaching engagement is coming to an end. If you've read this far, thank you.

It's often difficult to end a coaching engagement, for both coach and client. We've partnered closely for months, dug in deep, struggled through changes. Everyone wants to hang on a bit longer, yet we know it's time.

Clients leave with the satisfaction of having completed a big project. They know they've worked hard to accomplish something difficult. As a very recent client said to me, his grin so broad it was trying to escape his face, "This was the best thing I've done professionally." You think his coach wasn't thrilled to hear that?

I know your experience of coaching hasn't always been easy.

- You put your reputation on the line.

- You made yourself vulnerable.
- You tried new behaviors.
- You were willing to look foolish.
- You took some hard falls.
- You stuck with it when you had other urgent priorities.
- You kept coming back even when being coached was uncomfortable.
- You pushed beyond your doubts that you could ever really change.

For your efforts, you've made progress.

- You've decided what you wanted to accomplish.
- You've extracted the best of formal and informal feedback.
- You're getting it done.
- You think differently.
- You act differently.
- You've broken unhelpful habits.
- You're changing both from the outside in and the inside out (change that will last!).
- You're gaining competence in areas vital to you and your future.
- You've grown new confidence.
- You took charge of your engagement.

- You've mastered the coaching process.
- You maximized this experience.

You've made it. Crossed the finish line. Broken the tape!

Relish this! Don't forget to celebrate your accomplishments. Pop a bottle of champagne. Walk around the lake. Take a nap. Enjoy a nice dinner. Buy yourself a plaque. Whatever you do to memorialize completing a big task, do it!

CONGRATULATIONS!

Run On

Underneath, you're maybe still a little anxious. When your coaching sessions wind down, you'll run on your own, without a buddy. You don't want to waste the time, effort, and money you've invested just to fall back to the old status quo. Without the discipline and accountability of regular meetings, that would be all too easy.

How do you keep it all going—and make even more progress?

I have a couple suggestions.

First, just as you created a plan for the last six months, map out your steps for the next six months. You can use the structure I provide below. Coming up with this plan is so crucial that I use the last meeting or two with my clients almost solely for this purpose.

The first part of the plan looks back. By pausing and reflecting, you'll integrate the learning—embed it—into the new you. Ask yourself the following key questions:

- What big takeaways did I gain from assessments? From stakeholder interviews? From other feedback?

- What did I hope to accomplish? What did I choose to focus on?

- What actions did I take? What new behaviors did I try?

- What habits did I try to change?

- What worked for me? What didn't?

- What impact did I see from the changes I made?

- How did my outcomes compare to my desires or expectations?

Sustainable development plan for _____

Key insights from feedback	Actions - new leadership practices & behaviors	Impact of these new practices

Then, look forward. What do you want to work on during the next six months? It might be more of the same, adding additional steps, or working on entirely new areas you didn't get to the first time around. To make this concrete, list actions steps.

Here are the key questions:

- Looking forward, what is most important to me?
- In what areas do I want to continue making progress?
- What new areas do I want to address? Which have the highest priority?
- What might get in my way? How will I deal with that?
- What actions do I want to take?
- What resources do I need?

Sustainable development plan (p.2) for _____

Feedback on progress	Development areas going forward	Key action steps

Your new six-month plan not only gives you a sense of accomplishment and closure but a way to sustain and build on your progress.

Real Winning

Thank you for joining me on this journey. It's a true privilege to work with amazing people like you on things you value so highly.

My wish for you is to savor these moments of human connection, of learning, the raggedness of saw-toothed growth. And I wish that, as you learn and grow and occasionally fall down, you're gentle with yourself and pick yourself up with a smile.

> **Winning doesn't always mean being first. Winning means you're doing better than you've ever done before.**
> – Bonnie Blair

Appendix

Coaching Session Preparation Questions

Use these questions to reflect and prepare for your coaching session:

- How am I right now? How has my week gone?

- What do I want to get from my coaching session?

- Debrief of previous session.

    - What action(s) did I take since our last session? What were my wins or challenges? If I had "homework" how did that go?

    - What do I have to report? What do I want to be held accountable for?

    - What issues do I want to delve into more deeply during our coaching session? What challenges, concerns, achievements, or areas of learning need to be addressed?

- What else do I want to bring up?

360 Interview Questions

Purpose of 360 interview

1. Obtain feedback for XX as part of a coaching/development program.

2. Will preserve confidentiality. Will consolidate feedback and summarize themes. Won't disclose who said what.

3. Appreciate your time and candor in advance.

Introductions

What is your role? What is your relation to XX (peer, DR, boss, other?) How long have you known XX? How long have you been with the organization?

Questions

1. What do you see as XX's top strengths as a leader? Most significant weaknesses?

2. On a 1-10 scale, how do you rate XX as a leader? Why that number? What would raise his/her score higher?

3. What do you wish XX would start doing or stop doing as a leader—a change that would have the biggest impact on his/her effectiveness?

4. Does XX have a blind spot as a leader he/she should be aware of? Does he/she have any derailment issues?

5. Have you given XX feedback on his/her leadership? How did he/she respond?

6. How effective is XX at influencing others? What does he/she do well? Where can he/she improve? How well is XX navigating in the organization matrix?

7. How well has XX developed and articulated a strategic direction?

8. How strong has XX's execution been?

9. Has XX done what he/she needs to with respect to his/her organization, team, and direct reports?

10. How well does XX listen?

11. How aware of and sensitive to individuals' needs and perspectives is XX?

12. How does XX react when thing go wrong or mistakes are made? When the pressure is on? Does XX control emotions or wear them on his/her sleeve?

13. How would you assess the quality of XX's relationships with the team, peers and colleagues, others?

14. How effective is XX at communicating and keeping people informed?

15. Tell me about XX's integrity.

16. How effective is XX at delivering tough feedback?

17. How effective is XX at handling conflict? What makes you say that?

18. Tell me about XX's decision-making style. How effective is this?

19. How effective is XX at managing up? Sideways? Down?

20. Describe XX's executive presence.

21. Tell me about XX's platform skills. How effective is XX as a speaker? Tell me about different audiences. Does XX have any habits which distract from presentations?

22. What one or two things should XX do in the short-term that would most make a difference in his/her effectiveness?

Development Plan Review Meeting – Draft Agenda

Purpose

Discuss the leader's feedback, development plan objectives, and planned actions in a three-way meeting with the leader, the leader's manager, and the coach. Objective is to agree on the objectives and the action plan.

Agenda

- Purpose of meeting
- Roles of each attendee
- Review summary of feedback from assessments and discuss (might send in advance)
- Review draft development plan objectives and planned actions and discuss/obtain input
- Identify areas of agreement and areas of disagreement or gaps, if any
- Reach agreement on final development plan
- Requests from one another to aid success with the plan
- Potential next steps in coaching process
  - Coaching to the plan
  - Communication
  - Follow up toward end of engagement

Sample Coaching Agreement

> Agreement between COMPANY NAME
>
> and Meyer Partners, LLC
>
> Coaching Engagement—CLIENT NAME
>
> DATE

Engagement Context & Purpose

COMPANY NAME has engaged Mike Meyer of Meyer Partners, LLC to coach CLIENT NAME AND TITLE. This coaching engagement is expected to commence by DATE and will conclude approximately XX months later, on DATE. COMPANY NAME is the Sponsor of this engagement and is responsible for all fees and expenses associated with it. CLIENT NAME is the Client for this engagement. Mike Meyer of Meyer Partners, LLC, is the Coach for this engagement.

Coach will use appropriate coaching approaches, tools, and methodologies during this engagement. The objectives of the engagement are:

- Give feedback to Client on leadership and interpersonal style.

- Work with Client to create a comprehensive development plan and support him/her in making significant progress on agreed upon opportunities for professional development.

- Protect against Client's "derailment" by creating awareness of problems and developing new approaches to his/her leadership challenges.

Appendix

The Coaching Process

There are four phases of this coaching process: 1) Outcomes 2) Assessment 3) Development Action Plan and 4) Ongoing Coaching and Results.

PHASE 1: Outcomes

The initial phase is intended to lay the groundwork for the engagement. During this phase, outcomes will be discussed with boss, client, and coach. A review of the Client's role, as well as organization strategy, priorities, and culture will be completed. An initial assessment and coaching plan will be completed as well. Goal of this phase is to gain alignment on the plan and anticipated development focus areas.

PHASE 2: Assessment

The purpose of this phase is to complete a rigorous analysis of Client's leadership style and approach, and understand and create awareness of strengths and development needs, including potential "blind spots" which may be impeding performance. There will be a review of previous assessments such as performance feedback, 360, and other assessments. This phase may also include additional assessments. The additional assessments potentially include a self-assessment such as XXXX, an online 360 assessment, and 360 interviews of up to 10 people, including boss, peers, and direct reports. The latter will be summarized to provide anonymous qualitative feedback to the Client to supplement the quantitative assessments, which together will provide a comprehensive, composite description of Client's leadership strengths and weaknesses.

PHASE 3: Create Development Action Plan

This phase includes creation of a detailed development plan by the Client. Components could include:

- Key challenges, priorities, and expectations
- Competencies required for success in role
- Client strengths
- Client development focus areas
- Potential actions for managing key stakeholder relationships
- Detailed action plan including steps, timetable, accountability

Once the plan is drafted, it will be finalized with appropriate stakeholders via facilitated meetings.

PHASE 4: Ongoing Coaching, Practice, and Results

Once the assessment has been completed and development-planning objectives have been finalized, the ongoing coaching meetings focus on progress on the development plan, learning and practicing new skills, and addressing questions, issues, concerns, and challenges along the way. Progress is monitored and feedback solicited to gauge results and make adjustments.

Consideration and Expenses

The total fee for this engagement is $XX to be invoiced and paid by Sponsor in two equal installments of $XX. One installment will be paid at the beginning of the engagement, one at the conclusion of the engagement.

Regular expenses such as the XXX assessments, materials, books, etc., will be billed at cost. Significant expenses beyond these expenses are not expected, but when anticipated will be discussed and agreed to in writing in advance by Sponsor, Client, and Coach, and billed at cost. As an independent contractor, Coach is responsible for all taxes associated with the fees for this engagement and Coach is not eligible to participate in any Sponsor compensation or benefit plans.

Term

The coaching engagement will commence on or near DATE, and will conclude approximately XX months later, on DATE. If Sponsor terminates the agreement prior to its completion the entire fee will become payable to Coach unless Coach has failed to deliver the specified services, in which case the fee will be pro-rated based on the length of service provided and the appropriate adjustment to the fee will be made. Should Coach terminate the agreement prior to its completion, the entire fee will be pro-rated for the length of service provided and the appropriate adjustment to the fee will be made.

Roles and Responsibilities

Coach's responsibilities include ensuring agreement with Client and Sponsor on parameters of the engagement, delivering professional coaching services as described in this agreement, providing feedback to Client, and keeping Sponsor informed as described in this agreement.

Client's responsibilities include attending coaching meetings, working with Coach to create and make progress on a professional development plan, openly sharing information on progress and challenges with Coach, and communicating progress with Sponsor as appropriate.

Sponsor's responsibilities include participating in this engagement as needed to develop Client, such as in meetings to discuss goals and progress.

Confidentiality

The key to a successful coaching engagement is confidentiality. It is imperative that all parties have the same understanding of what this means in the context of a coaching engagement. Specific expectations are as follows:

1. **Coaching Session Content.** Anything shared by the Client within the parameters of the coaching relationship is shared in confidence and will not be disclosed by the Coach. The only exceptions to this are when there are violations of the organization's code of ethics, violations of the law, or the potential that the Client poses a risk of harm to him/herself or others. In these situations, the Coach will report these concerns to the Sponsor, as appropriate.

2. **Information about the Sponsor Organization.** Within the boundaries of the law, the Coach must keep all business or organizational information confidential unless it is otherwise available to the public. The exception to this rule is that the Coach is required to reveal to the appropriate representatives of the Sponsor, and possibly to legal authorities, any information regarding illegal or unethical improprieties.

3. **Information about the Client.** This may include assessment data, development needs, action plan content, and the like. Coach and Client will agree on any information that will be shared, and how and with whom it will be shared. Aside from this, Coach will periodically inform Sponsor whether meetings are occurring as planned and whether there continues to be an active and productive coaching engagement.

Other

Only Coach will perform the services described in this agreement and Coach agrees not to assign any of these services to another firm or individual. This agreement contains the entire agreement and may not be modified except in writing by both Coach and Sponsor.

Thank you for the confidence you have placed in Meyer Partners for this engagement. Please indicate agreement by signing and dating below.

Signed: _____

Dated: _____

Meyer Partners, LLC., Mike Meyer, President

Signed: _____

Dated: _____

Company Sponsor

Coach Selection Tool

Area:	Coach 1:			Coach 2:		
Education	H	M	L	H	M	L
Experience	H	M	L	H	M	L
Chemistry questions	H	M	L	H	M	L
1. _____	H	M	L	H	M	L
2. _____	H	M	L	H	M	L
3. _____	H	M	L	H	M	L
4. _____	H	M	L	H	M	L
5. _____	H	M	L	H	M	L
6. _____	H	M	L	H	M	L
7. _____	H	M	L	H	M	L
8. _____	H	M	L	H	M	L
9. _____	H	M	L	H	M	L
10. _____	H	M	L	H	M	L
Mini-coaching session	H	M	L	H	M	L
Overall Evaluation	H	M	L	H	M	L

Reference Comments:

Appendix

Streamlined Development Plan

Development insights for _____

Key insights from feedback	Strengths	Blind spots, performance gaps, development areas	Potential development focus areas

Draft development plan for _____

Development goals	Specific development actions	Success metrics/timing	Results

Detailed Development Plan

NAME _____ DATE _____

Objective #1 (repeat for up to 3 objectives): _____

SPECIFIC ACTIONS WITH TIMING

Action	Timing/Milestones	Success Metrics
On the job		
Feedback		
Mentoring/role models		
Reading		
Training/workshops		

Potential obstacles/Plan to remediate: _____

Benefits of improvement: _____

Strengths to leverage: _____

Support needed: _____

Appendix

A Calendar for Reflection

Daily (3 minutes)

- What went well today? What didn't go well?
- What did I learn today?
- What new thing did I try today?
- What one thing will I do differently tomorrow?

Weekly (5 minutes)

- What progress did I make last week?
- What do I need to focus on this week?

Monthly (10 minutes)

- How am I doing on my learning objectives?
- What do I need to do to keep learning?

Quarterly (15 minutes)

- How am I doing on my development?
- What is most important going forward?

Annually (1 hour)

- Where do I stand relative to what matters to me?

- Where do I want to be a year from now and how do I get there?
- What do I need to do to manage my learning more effectively?

Every 2-3 years (2-4 hours)

- How do I stay connected to my deepest mission and purpose?
- Where should I invest my time and energy?
- Is it time for me to pivot or disrupt myself in some way?
- What is a bold move I can make?

Decadely (1 day)

- Who do I want to be?
- What values do I want to live by? How am I doing against them?
- What do I need to do in the next five years to accomplish what matters most?

Appendix

Ongoing Development Plan for End of Coaching Engagement

Sustainable development plan for _____

Key insights from feedback	Actions - new leadership practices & behaviors	Impact of these new practices

Sustainable development plan (p.2) for _____

Feedback on progress	Development areas going forward	Key action steps

Mini-360 Questions

In the following development areas, rate the progress of (Client's name) over the past several months.

Development area	Less effective	No change	More effective	No change needed	Not enough info
1	-3 -2 -1	0	+1 +2 +3		
2	-3 -2 -1	0	+1 +2 +3		
3	-3 -2 -1	0	+1 +2 +3		
4	-3 -2 -1	0	+1 +2 +3		

Strengths: Among the areas above, what has gone particularly well?

Weaknesses and blind spots: Among the areas above, what has not gone well?

Guidance: What counsel or suggestions do you have that would help with progress on these areas going forward?

Developmental Experiences Ideas

A starting place for ideas of on-the-job activities to develop in specific areas.

People management

- Temporary fill-in for an absence
- Mentor someone
- Help onboard a new employee
- Tutor someone
- Run meetings

Communication

- Make a speech
- Do a big presentation
- Toastmasters
- Create communication materials/scripts
- Represent the team at cross-functional meetings
- Key readings
- Find an editor/someone who is a good communicator to emulate/learn from

Project management

- Manage a project
- Improve a process
- Run a campaign
- Develop a new product or service

Strategic vision

- Participate in an enterprise-wide task force or committee
- Conduct a competitive review
- Create and communicate vision, mission, values, strategy for your group
- Shadow other leaders
- Attend other leaders' staff meetings
- Attend industry/trade conferences
- Key readings
- Customer interaction
- Switch roles from staff to line or line to staff

Business acumen

- Help launch a new initiative or program
- Be part of a turnaround

- Conduct a cost-benefit analysis

- Develop financial acumen through training, review of financial statements, and being mentored

- Build a business case for an investment

- Assume P&L responsibility

- Create/manage a budget

Acknowledgements

It turns out it's really hard to write a book. I guess that's why this one sat on a shelf for two years while I gathered the glucose I needed. But more than glucose, I needed the support of an incredible team who infused me with the strength and stamina to get this across the finish line.

For my entire career, my wife, Mary, has supported me in innumerable ways, listening to my tales of woe with understanding and acceptance. As this book unfolded, you provided many great suggestions.

My daughter, Mandy, and her beau, Justin, also incredibly insightful, have loaned me tools from their field of clinical therapy. Son, Jeremy, and his wife, Laura, are a constant inspiration, as are my parents, Rochelle and Ivan.

I met Kevin Johnson, my editor and book coach, through serendipity. You are an incredibly talented author and editor, and your creativity sparked my limp prose to life. In this marathon, you carried me across the finish.

Kevin also introduced me to Richard Dodson, like Kevin a published author. Richard and his team at Artisan amazed me. From design, art, and final edits, to printing and distribution, they took care of everything with thorough professionalism.

I thank the many coaches who have helped me with my second career in Executive Coaching. In particular, I'm grateful to George Dow, my coach for this transition, as well as Dave Wondra and Pete Berridge, two exceptional coaches who provided precious guidance as I was getting started, and Jeff Auerbach, who gave me my initial training at the College of Executive Coaching.

Profound gratitude to my friends at True North, who have provided moral support every step of my journey.

I thank Trish Olinger, HR and Talent Development leader at Kohl's and a terrific work partner. She asked the simple question that was the genesis for this book. "Mike," you asked, "how can our executives get more out of coaching?"

I've been fortunate to have worked for many amazing leaders. Bill Dempsey, retired from Abbott; Rick Gonzalez, CEO at AbbVie; and Doug Baker, CEO at Ecolab are all world class.

And of course, I thank my hundreds of clients, past and present. I've learned more from you than you will ever learn from me. It's for you that I keep running.

Made in the USA
Coppell, TX
18 May 2021